"I would encourage everyone in the
at hand. Jerr Boschee's insights into
self-sufficient in order to do more m
to run a successful nonprofit today."

– **JIM WESTALL**, Fo

"Jerr Boschee is spot on with his consistent ability to drive right to the most timely and important challenges (and opportunities) within the evolving practice of entrepreneurship for the common good. Jerr has always focused on separating the ideal from the doable. This book is a must read for those who understand sustainable change-making is what impact is all about."

– **TOM REIS**, Program Director, W. K. Kellogg Foundation

"For anyone seriously considering a foray into social enterprise, this guide is an important point of departure. Filled with the accumulated experience of many practitioners, it offers valuable perspective from those who have 'been there and done that.' No one has a track record like Jerr Boschee, and we all benefit from his generosity in sharing it."

– **BILLY SHORE**, author of *Revolution of the Heart* and *The Cathedral Within*

"A must-read. Even the most entrepreneurial sector leaders will benefit from this book's clear and practical insight about achieving true sustainability."

– **JUDITH E. ALNES**, Executive Director, MAP for Nonprofits

"*Migrating from Innovation to Entrepreneurship* is a welcome addition to the field, a practical toolkit of critical concepts and principles that are based on Jerr's broad pioneering background and the experiences of other leading social entrepreneurs. You won't find a distillation of on-the-ground experience like this anywhere else!"

– **TOM WHITE**, Editor and Publisher, *Social Enterprise Reporter*

"This book should be in easy arm's reach of every nonprofit CEO and Board chair."

– **PROF. NORMAN DOLCH**, Louisiana State University in Shreveport

"The lexicon and bibliographies in this book are alone worth the price!"

– **KATHLEEN E. BUESCHER**, President/CEO, Provident Counseling, Inc., Saint Louis

"Coming from someone who has 'walked the walk,' Jerr Boschee's commentary is a wise and necessary wake-up call for donors and nonprofit practitioners to move from 'dreaming' to 'building' more sustainable organizations. As he so rightly points out: 'It is one thing to create and nurture a new program – and quite another to sustain it.' Hopefully this book represents the end of the debate over terminology and the migration from a focus on supporting *individual innovators* toward a more holistic approach to building stronger and more entrepreneurial social change *organizations*."

– **LEE DAVIS & NICOLE ETCHART**, Co-founders and CEOs, NESsT

"An important compass for community foundations as they explore meaningful ways to work with donors and nonprofits on the vital topic of social entrepreneurship."

– **JAN KREAMER**, Retired President and CEO, Greater Kansas City Community Foundation

"Jerr's command of the intricacies, pitfalls and practical realities of social entrepreneurship is both compelling and inspiring, as is his wise and thoughtful advice for those risk takers willing to commit their careers and organizations to a better future. This book, especially its Practical Lexicon for Social Entrepreneurs, will surely be a dog-eared companion for every new and engaged social entrepreneur in the United States and internationally."

– **TONY WAGNER**, President, International Federation of Settlements and Neighborhood Centers

"Concise and pragmatic – a wonderful overview of the often confusing world of social enterprise. For anyone wanting a short but on target clarification of social enterprise, its evolution, characteristics and purpose, this is just the tool."

– **KATIE BURNHAM LAVERTY**, Founder and President, The Society for Nonprofit Organizations, and Publisher, *Nonprofit World*

"Jerr Boschee draws on his decades of deep and pioneering involvement with social entrepreneurship to provide a powerful set of insightful and practical guidelines."

– **PROF. JAMES E. AUSTIN**, Co-Founder, Social Enterprise Initiative, Harvard Business School

"Jerr Boschee's long history of involvement in the field and his exposure to so many successful social enterprises have made him keenly aware of the critical success factors he details for social entrepreneurs."

– **RICH GILMARTIN**, President and CEO, Gulf Coast Enterprises; former President, The Americas Group–Workability international

"Clarifies the essential elements of becoming a successful social entrepreneur – a valuable summary for nonprofit leaders considering earned income strategies to accomplish their social mission."

– **MIKE BURNS**, President, Pioneer Human Services

"Jerr Boschee's long experience guiding social enterprises qualifies him to bring us this insightful overview. The hard won wisdom of social entrepreneurs and their advisors will save many from false starts and help others toward sustainable profits."

– **JOHN RIGGAN**, Founder and Retired Chair, TCCGroup, and Co-Founder, Social Enterprise Alliance

"My first reaction was 'Oh no, not another tome on social entrepreneurship!' But I read it – and hey!! – it is an interesting and informative essay, quite cogent and presented in a nice, compact manner."

– **PETER GOLDBERG**, President and CEO, Alliance for Children & Families

Migrating from innovation to entrepreneurship

How nonprofits are moving toward sustainability and self-sufficiency

Jerr Boschee

Founder and Executive Director
The Institute for Social Entrepreneurs

ENCORE! PRESS
MINNEAPOLIS, MINNESOTA | 2006

A slightly different version of the title essay in this book also appears in *Social Entrepreneurship: New Paradigms of Sustainable Social Change,* a collection of essays published by Oxford University Press. The lexicon for social entrepreneurs and the selected bibliography have been prepared specifically for this publication.

Much of the material on pages 9–16 has been developed jointly with Jim McClurg, Vice President of the Social Enterprise Alliance.

ISBN: 0-9777510-3-1

Library of Congress Control Number: 2006900019

Publishing advisor: Linda S. Ball, President, Publishing That Matters, Inc.

Designer: Sarah Anondson

This book is dedicated
to social entrepreneurs everywhere

For information about purchasing single copies, bulk discounts and Jerr Boschee's seminars, workshops and other publications:

The Institute for Social Entrepreneurs
9560 Dogwood Circle
Eden Prairie, Minnesota 55347-3028
United States of America

Web site: www.socialent.org
E-mail: institute@orbis.net
Telephone: +01-952-942-7715
FAX: +01-952-942-8059

Table of Contents

Dependency

The traditional business model for nonprofits, in which they depend solely or almost entirely on charitable contributions and public sector subsidies, with earned income either non-existent or minimal

Sustainability

The ability to fund the future of a nonprofit through a combination of earned income, charitable contributions and public sector subsidies

Self-sufficiency

The ability to fund the future of a nonprofit through earned income alone

Social entrepreneur

Any person, in any sector, who runs a social enterprise

Social enterprise

Any organization, in any sector, that uses earned income strategies to pursue a double or triple bottom line, either alone (as a social sector business) or as part of a mixed revenue stream that includes charitable contributions and public sector subsidies

SECTION ONE

Migrating from innovation to entrepreneurship

Introduction

Social innovators around the world have begun to reach a disquieting conclusion: Inspired vision, impassioned leadership, enthusiastic volunteers, government subsidies and a phalanx of donors are not always enough.

They serve admirably while innovators transform their dreams into fledgling programs and steer their organizations through early growing pains. But there comes a time, albeit reluctantly, when most founders and their followers begin to understand that living from year to year does not ensure the future, and that is the moment when they begin migrating from innovation to entrepreneurship. It is one thing to design, develop and carry out a new program, quite another to sustain it. So they begin turning toward commercial markets, gradually exploring the possibilities of *earned* income, many for the first time, and often with reluctance given their uneasiness about the profit motive.

The moment of realization comes at different stages and for different reasons. Major funders may be experiencing donor fatigue. The initial band of dedicated volunteers and employees might be burning out. Government support for a project could be waning or the cost of delivering services escalating dramatically. It might even be that the organization is on the threshold of significant growth but cannot proceed without new sources of financing.

In the United States, the moment arrived for most nonprofits in the mid- to late-1990s, although a handful of pioneering social entrepreneurs had been emphasizing earned income since the 1960s and 1970s. Around the world, the moment is dawning today for some of the most successful social innovators, and they are slowly moving away from a *dependency* model of financing that relies almost entirely on charitable contributions and public sector subsidies. The movement takes two forms:

- Some are working toward *sustainability*, which can be attained through a *combination* of philanthropy, subsidies and earned revenue

- Others are seeking *self-sufficiency*, which can only be achieved through earned revenue alone

However, entering commercial markets poses significant challenges for non-governmental organizations (NGOs), and the purpose of this essay is to review some of the lessons learned during the past 30 years by nonprofits in the United States that have turned increasingly toward earned revenue – nonprofits whose successes and failures serve as both models and cautionary tales for others.

The essay will:

- Summarize six historical forces that led to the emergence of social entrepreneurship in the United States

- Describe five basic principles that have evolved over time

- Present two unexpected outcomes experienced by nonprofits adopting entrepreneurial strategies

- Identify four types of stakeholder objections

- Analyze the single greatest obstacle encountered by entrepreneurial nonprofits

- Review 14 critical success factors emphasized by the pioneers in the field

Historical Context

The pressures on nonprofits in the United States began to build more than two decades ago. Six of the most damaging have been the following:

- *Depleted reserves:* During the late 1970s, the American economy simultaneously suffered recession and double-digit inflation. The pressures led to sharply escalating costs and tighter budgets for all nonprofits, the first sign that times were changing. During the next few years, the impact worsened: A national survey in 1977 showed that the average nonprofit had approximately three months of operating capital in reserve at the end of the year; the same survey 10 years later revealed that average capital reserves had fallen to less than four days.[1]

- *Diminished support from the public sector:* Driven by the Reagan Administration's emphasis on privatization, federal and state spending on social services and the arts began plummeting in the early 1980s, eventually falling by more than 23 per cent in a single decade.[2]

- *Reduced giving by individuals and corporations:* Changes in the tax code in 1986 also precipitated a substantial drop in giving from wealthy Americans, who by 1990 were donating only four per cent of their annual income to charity compared to seven per cent in 1979.[3] A parallel reduction in corporate philanthropy exacerbated the plunge – it failed to keep pace with inflation for six consecutive years after the tax code changes.[4] Overall, the relationship of private contributions to the current operating expenses of nonprofits in the United States shifted dramatically: In 1960, they covered 59.8 per cent, in 1990 only 31.5.[5] And, by 1997, private giving to human service organizations had fallen to its lowest point in 30 years.[6]

- *More competition for grants and contributions:* The number of 501(c)(3) charitable organizations in the United States has exploded. For every two that existed in 1977, there are more than five today[7], and they are all appealing to the same potential donors. As one frustrated Foundation executive put it, "there are just too damn many nonprofits out there, and they're tripping over each other."

- *More people in need:* By 1992, one in seven Americans were living below the poverty line,[8] including more than one in five children,[9] and 18 per cent of families with at least one adult holding a full-time job were still classified as living in poverty.[10] Beyond that, nonprofits were wrestling with an eruption of new challenges, including HIV/AIDS, homelessness, crack babies and an exponential growth in the number of frail elderly persons. According to Catholic Charities USA, four times as many people were seeking help from its member agencies in 1991 than just ten years previously; even more dismaying, only one in four needed help with basic food and shelter in 1981 – ten years later it was two out of three.[11]

- *A frayed reputation:* A series of scandals throughout the 1990s also caused many Americans to lose confidence in the sector, including misappropriation of funds by the head of the United Way of America, the nation's largest fundraising body; a pyramid scheme that stole more than $50 million from wealthy philanthropists; and embezzlement in the highest ranks of the Episcopal Church. As a result, by 1996, a national poll revealed that only 60 per cent of Americans believed charities were honest and ethical in their use of funds.[12]

These and other pressures impinging on nonprofits in the United States are familiar to NGOs around the world. They pose a daunting challenge, and earned income strategies have become an important part of the response.

Basic Principles

Social entrepreneurs in the United States have identified five basic principles that are fundamental to understanding entrepreneurship for NGOs.[13] In addition to the distinction between "sustainability" and "self-sufficiency" described on page 4, they include the differences between

- "Entrepreneurship" and "innovation"
- "Entrepreneurship" and "*social* entrepreneurship"
- "Earned income strategies" and "social sector businesses"
- "Innovators," "entrepreneurs" and "professional managers"

"Entrepreneurship" versus "innovation"

"Entrepreneurship" is one of the most misunderstood terms in the social sector today. Everybody, it seems, has a different definition of what it means.

Twenty years ago the idea of NGOs acting in an entrepreneurial manner was anathema to most people in the sector: The idea of merging mission and money filled them with distaste. But the phrase "social entrepreneur" is bandied about freely these days. British Prime Minister Tony Blair praises the emerging tide of "social entrepreneurs" that is changing the face of England's voluntary and community sector. Senior executives associated with Independent Sector, the national lobbying organization for nonprofits in the United States, talk about "social entrepreneurs" who find new and exciting ways to attract contributions and government support for their programs. Both are right to praise the ingenuity of NGOs – but most of what they are praising has nothing to do with entrepreneurship.

Here is the gist of the problem: Unless an NGO is generating *earned* revenue from its activities, it is *not* acting in an entrepreneurial manner. It may be doing good and wonderful things, creating new and vibrant programs . . . but it is *innovative*, not *entrepreneurial.*

Why is the distinction so important?

Because only earned income will ever allow an NGO to become truly sustainable or fully self-sufficient. Innovation is a precious resource and it served as the primary engine of nonprofit growth in the United States throughout the 1970s and 1980s. But innovation can take an NGO only so far. It is one thing to create and nurture a new program – and quite another to sustain it without depending on charitable contributions and public sector subsidies. Smart NGO managers and Board members realize they must increasingly depend on themselves to insure their survival – and that leads them naturally to the world of entrepreneurship.

However, too many NGO executives and trustees continue to use old methodologies and old definitions to gussy up their books and their brochures. It has reached the point where almost everything new in the social sector is called "entrepreneurial" and the people who create these new approaches (not to mention the people who write about them and underwrite them) walk away satisfied they have changed the fundamental equation.

They have not.

"Entrepreneurship" versus "social entrepreneurship"

According to Webster, an entrepreneur is "a person who organizes and manages a business undertaking, assuming the risk *for the sake of profit*."[14] In a 1998 column for *Inc.* magazine, Norm Brodsky expanded on the definition. "Starting with nothing more than an idea or a prototype," he wrote, "entrepreneurs have the ability to take a business to *the point at which it can sustain itself on internally generated cash flow*."[15]

The italics in both definitions have been added for emphasis, because successfully running a business means sustaining it with *earned* income, not grants or subsidies.

The most commonly quoted definition of "social entrepreneurship" today was formulated by Prof. J. Gregory Dees of Stanford University in 1998, but his essay contained a fundamental oversight. He outlines five factors that define social entrepreneurship: Adopting a mission to create and sustain social value (not just private value); recognizing and relentlessly pursuing new opportunities to serve that mission; engaging in a process of continuous innovation, adaptation, and learning; acting boldly without being limited by resources currently in hand; and exhibiting a heightened sense of accountability to the constituencies served and for the outcomes created.[16]

He never mentions earned income.

This is not only conceptually flawed, but also psychologically crippling. It lets NGOs off the hook. It allows them to congratulate themselves for being "entrepreneurial" without ever pursuing genuine sustainability or self-sufficiency. They still return, year after year, to individual donors, foundations and government agencies.

Without self-generated revenue, NGOs remain forever dependent on the generosity of others, and that is a risk social entrepreneurs are unwilling to take. They are passionately committed to their mission – but they are just as passionately committed to becoming financially sustainable or self-sufficient *in order to do more mission!* As traditional sources of funding dried up or became less available during the 1980s and 1990s, a growing number of nonprofits in the United States discovered the importance of paying their own way – and their managers became genuine social entrepreneurs who understood the difference between "innovation" (doing something new) and "entrepreneurship" (doing something that makes money). Over time, they transformed their nonprofits into social enterprises, using earned income strategies either alone (in a social sector business) or as part of a mixed revenue stream that also included charitable contributions and public sector subsidies.

What, then, *is* social entrepreneurship? And how does it differ from entrepreneurship *per se*?

To begin with, *a social entrepreneur is any person, in any sector, who runs a social enterprise*, and a social entrepreneur differs from a traditional entrepreneur in two important ways:

- Traditional entrepreneurs frequently act in a socially responsible manner: They donate money to NGOs; they refuse to engage in certain types of businesses; they use environmentally safe materials and practices; they treat their employees with dignity and respect. All of this is admirable, but their efforts are only *indirectly* attached to social problems. Social entrepreneurs are different because their earned income strategies are tied *directly* to their mission: They either start "affirmative businesses" (known as "social firms" in the United Kingdom) that employ people who are developmentally disabled, chronically mentally ill, physically challenged, poverty-stricken or otherwise disadvantaged; or they sell products and services that have a direct impact on a specific social problem (*e.g.*, delivering hospice care, working with potential dropouts to keep them in school, manufacturing assistive devices for people who are physically disabled, providing home care services to help elderly people stay out of nursing homes).

- Secondly, traditional entrepreneurs are ultimately measured by financial results: The success or failure of their companies is determined by their ability to generate profits for their owners. On the other hand, social entrepreneurs are driven by *a double bottom line*, a virtual blend of financial and social returns. Some pursue a *triple bottom line*, adding environmental returns to the mix. In either case, financial returns are still a goal, but not the only goal, and any profits that do result are often re-invested in the mission rather than being distributed to shareholders.

"Earned income strategies" versus "social sector businesses"

Many NGO Board members and executives are daunted by the prospect of social entrepreneurship because they think it means starting a business venture, something few know how to do. But creating a social sector business is just one of the earned income strategies available to a social enterprise, and it differs substantially from the others in terms of expectations and structure.

- *Earned income strategies:* Every NGO has opportunities for earned income lying fallow within its existing programs. One or two might be candidates for conversion into social sector businesses, but most will be tiny and never have the potential for profitability. Nevertheless, exploiting them can have significant cumulative impact. By aggressively turning inward and searching for pockets of existing opportunities, social enterprises have been able to register impressive gains, often raising their percentage of total revenue from earned income by as much as 15 per cent within one to three years, a considerable boon to sustainability.

- *Social sector businesses:* Once a social enterprise has successfully carried out a variety of earned income strategies, it may want to consider launching a social sector business – but the goals would be much more ambitious and the strategy completely different. The *only* reason for a social enterprise to start a social sector business is to exploit a *specific* opportunity for significant growth and profitability – a substantial difference from other earned income strategies, which are designed primarily to cover more of a program's costs, without any real expectation of making a profit or even reaching a break-even point. The pioneers in the field have also discovered that the chances for success with a social sector business increase dramatically if the social enterprise creates a "skunk works," a completely separate entity insulated as much as possible from the day-to-day operations of the parent organization. That means having a separate staff, separate compensation policies and, if necessary, even a separate Board of Directors in order to achieve as much independence as possible.

"Innovators," "entrepreneurs" and "professional managers"

Perhaps the single most important lesson learned by the pioneers in the field has been a deeply personal one that strikes to the very heart of their self-perceptions. So often, NGOs discover (too late) that their entrepreneurial efforts have been doomed simply because they are being led by people with the wrong types of skills. The mistake occurred because they did not truly understand the differences between innovators, entrepreneurs and professional managers.

Regardless of whether an NGO is attempting to maximize earned income internally or trying to launch a social sector business, it is important to understand the differences between the three types of leaders: They are all needed in the evolution of a healthy organization, but at different times, and rarely does an individual excel in more than one of the three areas.

Innovators are the *dreamers*: They create the prototypes, work out the kinks – and then get bored, anxious to return to what they do best, which is inventing more prototypes. They are rarely concerned, ultimately, with the long-term financial viability of what they do.

Entrepreneurs are the *builders*: They turn prototypes into going concerns – then *they* get bored. For them, financial viability is the single most important aspect of what they do.

Professional managers are the *trustees*: They secure the future by installing and overseeing the systems, standards and infrastructure needed to make sure the going concern keeps going.

Unfortunately, often because resources are scarce, NGOs try to shoehorn people into positions where they don't fit, and many of the problems they have when they begin adopting entrepreneurial strategies arise from having an innovator or a professional manager trying to do an entrepreneur's job.

Potential Outcomes

> "The beauty of making a profit, as we've been able to do during the past 15 years, is that you can do *a lot* with the money, you can do what *you* want to do. You can do it *how* you want to do it for as *long* as you want to do it and you don't have to make *anybody* happy except your own Board and staff. You don't have to meet anybody else's expectations. That's a very freeing idea, and once you feel it, you don't want to go back to the confines of any other type of funding."
>
> *Kathleen Buescher, President and Chief Executive Officer, Provident Counseling, Inc., St. Louis, Missouri*

When they began entering the commercial markets, social entrepreneurs in the United States were primarily interested in finding new sources of revenue to help them maintain and expand their programs, but they quickly discovered there was much more to gain than financial returns. In addition to obtaining the freedom described by Kathleen Buescher, two of the most important results have been learning how to sharpen their strategic focus and becoming a more powerful voice for the people they serve.

New strategic directions

The concept of "organized abandonment" began to seep into the United States nonprofit sector during the late 1980s when management guru Peter Drucker turned his attention to the field and recoiled from what he saw. Too many nonprofits were becoming increasingly unwieldy, unable to give their clients the attention they deserved because they no longer had the necessary time or resources. And much of the pain was self-inflicted: Multi-service organizations were growing frenetically, adding programs every year, spreading themselves thinner and thinner. Drucker had some blunt advice: If your products or services are not number one or number two in the market, kill them. Rather than trying to be all things to all people, concentrate on doing the best job possible in a few, carefully chosen areas.[17]

Drucker's advice runs against the grain of the traditional NGO mentality, but most NGO managers eventually do admit they are trying to serve too many masters, and his suggestion gives them a lifeline, a way to simultaneously sharpen their organizational focus and expand their impact. However, the process can be agonizing. It is not easy to kill programs, especially if they are the pet projects of Board members or funders. And there *is* an important caveat: Organized abandonment for NGOs does *not* mean eliminating a program just because it fails to generate earned revenue: If the NGO is the best or only provider of a program that is critically needed, it has a compelling reason to continue the program – and a managerial challenge to find other sources of revenue to cover the cost.

In effect, entrepreneurs in the nonprofit sector in the United States during the 1980s and 1990s discovered a stunning irony: The first rule of entrepreneurship is contraction. And one of the decision-making tools they have been using has been "The Organized Abandonment Grid"® *(Figure 1)*, which enables them to *simultaneously* analyze the social impact and financial viability

Figure 1: "The Organized Abandonment Grid"®

Notes: "Profits" and "losses" are for annual operations and include all direct and indirect costs; "profits" are pre-tax and prior to capital re-investment

FINANCIAL VIABILITY				SOCIAL PURPOSE: CRITICAL 5	SIGNIFICANT 4	SOME 3	MINIMAL 2	NONE 1
	PROFITS	21% OR MORE	7	DEFINITELY	DEFINITELY	DEFINITELY	PROBABLY	MAYBE
		11% - 20%	6	DEFINITELY	DEFINITELY	DEFINITELY	MAYBE	MAYBE
		0% - 10%	5	DEFINITELY	DEFINITELY	PROBABLY	MAYBE	PROBABLY NOT
	LOSSES	1% - 10%	4	PROBABLY	PROBABLY	PROBABLY	PROBABLY NOT	DEFINITELY NOT
		11% - 40%	3	PROBABLY	PROBABLY	MAYBE	DEFINITELY NOT	DEFINITELY NOT
		41% - 70%	2	MAYBE	MAYBE	PROBABLY NOT	DEFINITELY NOT	DEFINITELY NOT
		71% - 100%	1	MAYBE	PROBABLY NOT	DEFINITELY NOT	DEFINITELY NOT	DEFINITELY NOT

of each program and decide whether to keep it. Once the analysis has been completed, they can make rational decisions about which programs to expand, maintain, reduce, divest or eliminate.

At its heart, organized abandonment requires an NGO to be honest with itself – exceedingly difficult for any organization, NGO or otherwise. But the results have been worth it, and the ultimate winners have been the clients. Social entrepreneurs have discovered that reducing the number of programs they offer has actually enabled them to serve more people and to serve them better, because they have had the time and resources to expand their most effective and needed programs, to selectively launch innovative programs, to create new positioning strategies and marketing plans, and to develop profitable social sector businesses.

Speaking truth to power

Generating additional revenue, freeing themselves from the expectations of others, re-calibrating their strategic focus and serving more people are not the only benefits social entrepreneurs have derived from adopting earned income strategies or starting social sector businesses. There is another more subtle but just as seminal result.

In his keynote speech at The 4th National Gathering for Social Entrepreneurs in December 2002[18], Charles King told his audience about his recent trip to the international AIDS summit in Barcelona. "It became increasingly obvious during the conference," he said, "that if we are ever going to seriously address the plague of AIDS, it is not going to be government that leads the way, and it is not going to be corporations. If we are to make any significant progress, NGOs will have to lead the way." But he pointed out that most nonprofits are dependent on government subsidies and corporate largesse. How then, he asked, can they speak truth to power?

It was a powerful moment for his audience, because social entrepreneurship begins to loosen the chains of dependence. When the individuals and organizations that control the purse strings are also those that must step aside or change their practices, it becomes more difficult for NGOs to speak freely – but, as emphasized by Kathleen Buescher, when the purse strings are severed, the power relationships change.

Stakeholder Objections

The NGOs most prepared for entrepreneurship today are those that have been the most innovative during the past 10 or 15 years. Their challenge is to make the transition from a culture of innovation to a culture of entrepreneurship – but the path is strewn with dangers and the changes do not occur without a considerable shock to the system. Not every nonprofit is willing to take the necessary steps to complete the transformation: They are beset with nightmares, which typically fall into four categories.

Generic nightmares

Board members, staff members, clients, customers and other stakeholders have numerous misconceptions about earned revenue that rise quickly to the surface. They immediately ask questions such as these:

- How can we justify "making money off the backs of the poor"?
- What happens to quality when we emphasize financial returns?
- Will we have a two-tiered system that ignores people who can't afford to pay?

They reflexively believe pursuing earned income is "too risky," predict funders and other stakeholders will object, express concerns about liability exposures, bemoan the absence of models and expertise, and of course retreat behind the "not invented here" syndrome. In short, they have dozens of reasons not to proceed, including (quite often) a fundamental discomfort with making money.

Logistical nightmares

The "resource" question becomes an insurmountable stumbling block for many NGOs. Some of the logistical barriers include:

- Entrenched patterns of behavior
- Competing priorities
- Inadequate resources (dollars, people, time, psychic energy)
- Lack of business development, operations and marketing skills

However, the pioneers in the field have repeatedly demonstrated that when an NGO *really* wants to do something, it manages somehow to find the resources it needs: Being able to do so is almost the *sine qua non* of entrepreneurship.

The nightmare of failure

There are no guarantees, and the possibility of failure is very real. Personal careers can crash and burn. So NGO Board members and executives stew about the consequences: If we start down this path and fail, how can we avert a financial disaster? Will it damage our reputation? Can we do it without depleting our energy and resources?

Some of the other questions that plague them are these:

- Will we lose sight of our mission while trying to save it?
- Will we wind up shepherding bloated programs that never get anywhere (a different type of "failure")?
- What about opportunity cost? If we fail at this, we have really failed twice.
- What if it causes our best people to burn out or leave?
- How will funders react to future requests for help?
- What about lawsuits?
- Who will get the blame?

The nightmare of success

And there is still one more nightmare: Success itself. What happens when social entrepreneurs achieve their objectives? Simple: Somebody raises the bar. And the entrepreneurs find themselves grappling with questions like these:

- Can we continue to *care*? Or will we lose our hearts when we find our wallets? What about all the people who came to do good and stayed to do well?

- Can we manage rapid growth without overextending our resources?
- What happens if the market changes or the competition toughens or our best people are lured away?
- How will we deal with the inevitable ascending expectations placed upon us by ourselves and others?
- How can we avoid becoming complacent or lazy, resist trying to cover our mistakes with money rather than ingenuity?
- How can we make sure we do not lose control of our mission if we turn to outside investors to fuel our expansion plans?

All these nightmares cause many NGOs to spin their wheels, waiting for the perfect market opportunity, the perfect plan, the perfect time. None of them exist.

The Single Greatest Obstacle

The culture of a traditional NGO, no matter how innovative, is vastly different from the culture of an entrepreneurial NGO. Entrepreneurs have a higher tolerance for risk, a greater appreciation of margins, an eagerness to compete. Traditional NGOs distrust the capital markets, prefer collaboration to competition, and underestimate the productive capabilities of their disadvantaged employees. They watch other NGOs become increasingly sustainable or self-sufficient, but are unwilling to emulate their practices.

Instead, they criticize. "My god, the resistance," says Rick Walker, who runs seven small businesses in Marshfield, Massachusetts, that employ people with developmental disabilities. "To a great extent, nonprofit people are not risk-takers, and their unwillingness to think outside very standard parameters constantly amazes me. Quite frankly, we've had a lot better luck getting people outside the nonprofit world to understand what we're doing and feel comfortable with it."

Tony Wagner concurs. He has been astonished by the resistance he has encountered from both the business community and the nonprofit sector as his nonprofit in Minneapolis, Minnesota, tries to simultaneously create a business and carry out a social mission by employing people who are economically disadvantaged. "I've been blown away by the level of misunderstanding and mistrust," he says. "For all the writing and talking that's being done about the subject, out there in the world people either don't get it or don't want to get it. They say you have to be one or the other."

Why does this happen? Why is the embedded culture of an organization so often the single greatest obstacle for trustees and senior executives trying to launch earned income strategies or social sector businesses?

John Maxwell tells a wonderful story in his book *Failing Forward* that illustrates the problem:

> Four monkeys were placed in a room that had a tall pole in the center. Suspended from the top of that pole was a bunch of bananas. One of the hungry monkeys started climbing the pole to get something to eat, but just as he reached out to grab a banana, he was doused with a torrent of cold water. Squealing, he scampered down the pole and abandoned his attempt to feed himself. Each monkey made a similar attempt, and each one was drenched with cold water. After making several attempts, they finally gave up.
>
> Then researchers removed one of the monkeys from the room and replaced him with a new monkey. As the newcomer began to climb the pole, the other three grabbed him and pulled him down to the ground. After trying to climb the pole several times and being dragged down by the others, he finally gave up and never attempted to climb the pole again.
>
> The researchers replaced the original monkeys, one by one, and each time a new monkey was brought in, he would be dragged down by the others before he could reach the bananas. In time, the room was filled with monkeys who had never received a cold shower. None of them would climb the pole, but not one of them knew why.[19]

The plight of the monkeys resembles that of many NGOs: People continue doing things but have no idea why. Too many of them suffer from what Joel Arthur Barker calls "paradigm paralysis."[20] As Barker points out, paradigms can be extraordinarily useful. They help us make sense of the world by organizing incoming data streams and sorting them into categories, helping us decide what to think and do. But paradigms can be a double-edged sword. Blinders are slapped into place and we begin to interpret new information according to our pre-conceptions. We become frozen. Change becomes our enemy. Individuals and organizations begin to believe the categories they are using are the only ones available, and they slowly become paralyzed.

Institutional paralysis can be overcome, with a sufficient dose of courage. But occasionally it takes something dramatic. In the mid-1980s, when the Board of Directors of a nonprofit in Louisville, Kentucky, offered Bob Russell the job as CEO, he realized the existing make-up of the Board worked against entrepreneurship and agreed to accept the position only if every member of the board resigned. They agreed.

Still another CEO, who ran a sheltered workshop for people who were developmentally disabled, decided to change the basic values of his organization – and in the process invented an entirely new type of business, known today as an "affirmative business." On a pleasant summer evening in 1973, John DuRand invited his 11 senior managers to a downtown hotel in St. Paul, Minnesota, where he wined and dined them, asked them to sit down – and then fired them all. Five minutes later he passed out application forms. "Starting tomorrow," he said, "we are no longer a rehab agency, we're a business. Starting tomorrow, we no longer have clients, we have employees. And, starting tomorrow, you are no longer social workers, you are business managers. If you can get your minds and hearts and souls around that concept, I want you back. If you can't, I'll help you find a job somewhere else." Nine of the 11 returned to their jobs. Two could not accept the philosophic shift. But, from that day, the culture of the organization changed and the primary goal became the operation of a viable social enterprise.

However, regardless of dramatics, cultural change must be systemic.

The first step usually has to be taken at the Board level. When Charley Graham arrived at his new post in Oregon in the early 1980s, he immediately began promoting the idea of a double bottom line. According to his second-in-command, Roy Soards, "he told the Board we were never going to be able to employ more people with psychiatric disabilities if we continued operating a sheltered workshop and depending primarily on social service subsidies and charitable giving. He convinced the Board that if we provided quality goods and services, people would buy them and we'd therefore be able to employ even *more* people with disabilities and help them become self-sufficient."

Kevin McDonald, founder of a moving company in North Carolina that employs former convicts, drug addicts and prostitutes, found that customers appreciated the change. He built his company primarily through personal selling and word of mouth. "We didn't have a very big staff," he says, "just me and two others, and we didn't have much money for advertising. We were just trying to survive as a program. So, I decided to start hitting the pavement and gave a lot of speeches. Went out to the Junior League, the Kiwanis Club, that sort of thing . . . and I found they were tired of people asking for a handout. So I told them, 'I don't want your money . . . I want your *business* . . . call us up, let me give you an estimate . . . *use* our services.'"

Once they begin paying for actual products or services, customers become increasingly demanding, which puts a further strain on an organization's traditional culture. "When we started working with Ben & Jerry's," recalls Julius Walls, CEO of Greyston Bakery, which employs former convicts and others with barriers to employment, "they made it very clear that our product (providing brownies and blondies for five Ben & Jerry ice cream flavors) had to always be up to snuff or they wouldn't produce their ice cream with us. They held us accountable as a business and not as their young child. They provided a lot of assistance, but they told us from the beginning that we needed to stand up and be a business, not a sheltered workshop." When Walls took over the Yonkers, New York, company as CEO, he discovered that the biggest obstacle he faced was helping his employees "understand what we needed to do to be a sustainable model. We had to understand we were a business with a dual bottom line. Most businesses have one bottom line – economic dividends. (At the time) Greyston also had a single bottom line, but it wasn't the economic one. There was a mentality on the part of the employees that came here that if you're really nice we'll figure something out to keep you and it doesn't matter if you're producing or if the business is doing well. But there came a time when the employees and the business needed to understand that that's not a sustainable model."

The cultural transformation can turn into a war. "By the time I got here," remembers Soards, who eventually succeeded Graham as CEO in Oregon, "there was a demilitarized zone between the production people who ran the factory and the rehab people who provided social services. We had two very strong-willed managers and each of them had their own lieutenants and armies." The opposing forces fought over resources and, more fundamentally, they fought for the soul of the organization. It took years for the culture wars to subside, and "it was pretty ugly at times," says Soards. "The rehab people would sabotage the production people, who often had to rely on the rehab folks for employees. If the production people had a job that had to get done, they were under a lot of pressure, because the rehab people were more concerned about, 'Well, is this the proper training for this individual, they're not ready for work that's too demanding, and why don't you guys find the types of jobs that fit their needs, and no, they can't work after three o'clock because they have to go see their case workers.' We finally had to part ways with the head of the rehab division."

Hiring people from the for-profit world can be another wake-up call. "Everything changed," says Dave McDonough, who ran a social enterprise in Los Angeles that employed people who were homeless. "Right off the top, it was just the way the new people walked and talked and dressed and approached their day. It was a big shock to the rest of us."

Fundamentally, neither the traditional nonprofit approach nor the traditional for-profit approach works in a double bottom line environment. Please see "Crossing the Cultural Divide®" *(Figure 2)* for a depiction of the changes required to create a new, hybrid culture. Many of the elements in the chart are also reflected in the "critical success factors" discussed in the next section.

Figure 2: "Crossing the Cultural Divide"®

CATEGORY	TRADITIONAL NONPROFIT MENTALITY	TRADITIONAL FOR-PROFIT MENTALITY	HYBRID (SOCIAL ENTERPRISE) MENTALITY
Primary benchmark	Social returns	Financial returns	Double bottom line *(social and financial)*
Sine qua non	Year-to-year survival	Ongoing self-sufficiency	Ongoing sustainability
Primary stakeholders	Clients ("the people we serve")	Customers ("the buyers")	*Clients and customers*
Basic approach	Try to do it all	Capitalize on a niche	Focus on selected programs
Attitude toward earned income	Filthy lucre	Staff of life	Means to an end
Attitude toward making a profit	Uncomfortable, "illegitimate"	*Raison d'etre*	A tool for sustainability
Tolerance for R&D	Short-term *("cost")*	Long-term *("investment")*	Medium-term *("investment")*
Attitude toward taking risks *(in the commercial marketplace)*	Generally averse	Necessary evil	Reluctant but willing
Level of commitment when launching a business venture	Conflicted	Committed	Conservative but committed

CATEGORY	TRADITIONAL NONPROFIT MENTALITY	TRADITIONAL FOR-PROFIT MENTALITY	HYBRID (SOCIAL ENTERPRISE) MENTALITY
Strategic planning methodology	Mission-driven	Market-driven	Matrix-driven *(mission and market)*
Market research	All but non-existent	Extensive	Extensive
Segmentation of markets	Minimal	Extensive	Extensive
The "buyer"	Clients first, then funders	Customers	Customers first, then clients, then funders
Approach to marketing	Tactical	Strategic	Strategic
Determining quality standards	Nonprofit usually decides	Customers dictate	Customers and clients dictate
Organizational heirarchy	Fairly rigid	Very rigid	Less rigid
Decision-making process	Consensus	Heirarchical	Empowering
Executive compensation levels	Marginal	Competitive	Increasingly competitive
Employee financial incentives	Low risk, low reward	High risk, high reward	Risk-taking rewarded
Typical attitude toward non-performing employees	Forgiving	Harsh	Tough
Crisis fall-back options *(beyond expense reductions)*	Seek contributions	Acquire debt, sell equity, kill product or service lines	Seek contributions, acquire debt, sell equity, kill programs

Critical Success Factors

In addition to changing their organizational culture, the pioneers in the field have found that a significant number of other factors come into play. Here are 14 they believe are particularly important.

1. Candor

Entrepreneurs understandably fall in love with their business ideas – but love can be blind. Starting a new venture, or even an earned income strategy, is difficult enough without being honest about their product or service, their market, their competition, their resources. The mantra is very simple: "Beware of yourself!"

Tony Wagner discovered the power of candor the day two of his Board members took him aside. "It was probably the darkest day of my career," he recalls. "I'd gotten into this 'I can't fail' routine. I kept saying, 'Give me one more month and I'll make it work.' And I remember the Board meeting very clearly when two guys I respect very highly looked me right in the eye and said, 'Tony, it's over.' It wasn't until that point that I faced reality. As an entrepreneur, sometimes you just can't admit defeat. But I learned a valuable lesson. You need to have people outside you who aren't as passionate or emotionally involved who can ask the hard questions and say the things that need to be said."

Employees can also be among a social entrepreneur's greatest allies. Rich Gilmartin runs seven businesses in Florida that collectively generate more than $30 million in revenue and employ people who are disabled or disadvantaged. Over the years he has learned that some of his best problem solvers are his employees – *but only if they know that a problem exists.* "We were doing okay with one of our businesses," he recalls, "but we weren't generating the type of financial contribution we wanted. We were real close, but we were constantly in the red, so we resigned ourselves that things were as good as they were going to get. But one day the contract administrator who reports to me went to a meeting with our employees and laid it all out. We'd never done that before. The employees had never been told they were in the red – and when they heard about it they basically said, 'We can fix it!' It only took them four to six months to get us into the black." The experience prompted Gilmartin to open his books to all his employees. "We now have a very transparent policy," he says. "If employees want information about what's going on financially or how decisions are being made, we give it to them."

Candor is especially important as a company begins to expand. "You have to be careful," says Kevin McDonald. "We started growing so quickly our infrastructure couldn't keep up, so I had to slow things down. We had to be honest with ourselves and be cautious about which jobs to bid on rather than building up a reputation for biting off more than we could chew."

2. Clarity of purpose

What are the driving forces behind a decision to begin adopting or expanding entrepreneurial strategies? The members of an organization's entrepreneurial team must reach a consensus on this issue before they start the planning process *because they will be intensely scrutinized once they begin* and will need to have a consistent, compelling answer for their critics (and there *will* be critics!). Here are four rationale developed by a nonprofit in Minnesota:

- *Mission:* We will be able to serve more people
- *Survival:* Our traditional sources of funding are drying up
- *Opportunity:* The market is beckoning, already anxious to buy what we have
- *Freedom:* If we can generate more of our *own* money, we will not be so bound to the priorities and restrictions imposed on us by others

Those four words – mission, survival, opportunity and freedom – became the rallying cry for the organization's entire planning effort and a major reason for its long-term success.

But there is another aspect of clarity that is equally important, though it forces NGOs onto treacherous soil because circumstances change so rapidly, and that is the answer to the following question: "What will success look like?" It's important to define some concrete, long-term goals before getting started: They serve as a beacon and a source of energy – and without them social entrepreneurs can lose their way. Rich Gilmartin made sure his employees understood in 2000 that the company intended to grow from $13 million to $30 million within two years. "It was a big, hairy-assed goal," he laughs, "but we made it."

3. Courage

The typical NGO is plagued by crises: Unless the Board declares entrepreneurial planning a priority, it will be swept aside by the flood of day-to-day demands. Unfortunately, too many Boards are reluctant to commit because they are either risk-averse or searching for a quick fix. Both attitudes are understandable, but they conflict with marketplace realities.

The fact is, some earned income strategies and social sector businesses will fail. Unless the Board is willing to accept that fact and take some chances, it should not proceed at all. And the Board must also be willing to take a longer view: Too many members still think in terms of "cost" rather than "investment," and are therefore reluctant to proceed unless they can see a rapid return. Entrepreneurship does not typically work that way. It takes time. A ten-year study of 814,000 small businesses by the Massachusetts Institute of Technology (MIT) showed that significant revenue did not begin to flow until the seventh year.[21]

Rick Walker knew "we were heading into uncharted territory, so we formed a New Ventures Committee" 18 months before he launched his first business. "We had Board members, staff members, the people we served and their family members. We brought everybody together and talked about doing something that was very, very different from what any of us were used to doing in our job placement program or in our old sheltered workshop model." Walker believes the committee "instilled a sense of risk-taking across the organization" and set the tone that made it possible for an entire network of businesses to emerge.

Even now, years later, Walker minimizes his exposure by spreading his risks. "A lot of people say we're in too many businesses," he says, "but the issue for me is risk management.

Collectively, their impact is large – but each of them is small, so failure wouldn't be critical to the agency as a whole. The point is, *we need to be prepared to eat our mistakes*, and most nonprofits are not real good at that. For example, each of our little businesses is generating some revenue and creating some jobs, but if the ice cream store continues losing money because we're not able to solve our location problem, I'll kill it. We can't afford those kinds of losses. Or if the bookstore business goes completely kaflooey and starts doing terribly, I'm not going to let it imperil the agency as a whole. Or somebody could build a giant Motel 6 down the street and be better prepared to respond to the market. We don't have pockets deep enough to compete in a situation like that, so it means we'd fold our cards, close our motel and go off in a new direction."

Of the six businesses operated by Esperanza Unida that employ Latino members of the community in Milwaukee, Wisconsin, two are profitable, three are slightly under water and one is struggling. Over the past ten years, four others have come and gone, but Executive Director Richard Oulahan does not consider that a bad track record. "You *have* to take risks," he says. "Our community and our organization and our Board basically feel we don't have a lot of choice. If we're sitting here losing resources every day and people are being destroyed by our economic system, what do we have to lose if we go out on a limb and try to make something work? You can't be crazy. You've got to be careful. But there's nothing wrong with making mistakes. We've made a lot of them – but we look at them as a natural part of development and growth. Nothing gets done unless you make them! You try one thing and if it doesn't work you try something else. Any time you create something, there are always pieces on the ground around it when it's finished. So we're not afraid of mistakes. We just figure that something's always lost when you create something new."

"Nothin' surprises me any more," says Kevin McDonald. "I've been doin' this sort of thing for 20 years, and I was a street urchin before that. I just know that if you believe in something hard enough and work hard enough, it's gonna happen. You just don't quit no matter how hard it looks. You just keep goin' . . . ."

4. Core values

Critics often ask how it is possible to balance mission and money, to talk about moral imperatives and the profit motive in the same sentence. The answer lies in an organization's core values, a set of four or five basic principles that are clearly articulated, institutionalized, and constantly reinforced. In order for something to qualify as a "core" value, according to consultant Ronnie Brooks,

- An organization must be willing to accept the consequences
- The value must be freely chosen from genuine alternatives
- It must be acted upon as a regular pattern of action
- It must apply everywhere in the work
- It must last over time
- And the organization must be proud of it

Entering the world of entrepreneurship means an NGO will be confronted by temptations that have never appeared before and will need to maintain an internal sense of balance. The rules associated with core values are straightforward: Identify them before doing anything else; make sure they can be quantified; build them into strategic plans and annual operating plans; monitor them religiously; measure progress periodically; and trumpet results to the world.

Kevin McDonald says a core value in his company is that "our employees have to act in a professional manner. When you're dealing with recovering addicts, the first thing you have to do is make sure they're not using drugs. You can't be la-dee-dah about it. The accountability has to be there. You've gotta have discipline, and appearance is really important. Our people are taught to dress, speak and act professionally. Part of our goal is to change people's perceptions of addicts as street people, and sometimes our people forget that the customer is the person paying the bills. We have to go back to the basics. If somebody isn't performing, if they're disrespectful to a customer, we'll have to fire them."

One of the core values at Gulf Coast Enterprises is emphasizing to employees that they are responsible for *all* the company's resources. Essentially, says Rich Gilmartin, "we want our people to take ownership of both our tangible and intangible resources, regardless of their specific jobs. We don't want them thinking it's somebody else's responsibility. For example, in most organizations, if you see a visitor who appears to be lost, hopefully a staff member will give that person directions – but, in our system, the expectation is that you'll actually walk them to their destination, no matter what else is going on. That leaves a powerful impression."

The core values adopted in 1989 by The Affirmative Business Alliance of North America (now part of Workability International) and still in use today are as follows:

- Individuals with mental, physical, economic or educational disadvantages *are* capable of holding real jobs, *should* receive competitive wages, and *deserve* opportunities for career advancement and profit-sharing

- It *is* possible to operate successful businesses while employing substantial numbers of individuals who are disadvantaged

- The first priority of an affirmative business is to operate a viable business, not to employ a specific number of people

- Affirmative businesses treat their employees as employees, not as clients

5. Willingness to plan

According to the United States Small Business Administration, 90 per cent of business failures are caused by management mistakes, not by competitors, changes in the market or other external factors.[22]

Here are three suggestions offered by some of the pioneers in the field to get off on the right foot:

- *Ask for help:* Be sure the planning team includes some "business mentors," proven entrepreneurs who have successfully built their own small or medium-sized businesses. They will provide a reality check that is invaluable. Also, bring in some "wild cards," people who may not know much about the organization or even about business *per se*. Tell them their job is to ask all the "dumb" questions out loud, to probe the areas others might neglect because they are too close to the table.

- *Put somebody in charge:* The planning team needs to have a leader – a single person. Do not try to lead by committee – and do not ask somebody to be the leader in addition to his or her regular job: Without a dedicated focus, the process will drift.

- *Create a comfort zone:* Once the entrepreneurial team has been assembled, take some time to make sure everybody involved is comfortable with the organization's strategic framework, and that they know and agree on the answers to the following five questions:

    - What is our vision (how do we want the world to change)?

    - What is our mission (what will we do to bring about that change)?

    - What forces are driving us to adopt or expand earned income strategies?

    - What outcomes do we expect?

    - What core values will guide us?

Most NGOs find it worthwhile to spend one or two meetings at the beginning of the planning process clarifying the answers to these questions and are often surprised at what happens. The "mentors" and "wild cards" (and occasionally the insiders) challenge some of the organization's most dearly held assumptions – and many times the answers begin to change.

6. Building the right team

There are at least four critical components to building the right team for a successful social sector business:

- *The leader:* NGOs have historically made three critical mistakes when seeking a qualified leader for their business venture:

  - *Inadequate focus*: "We started by simply assigning the project as an additional set of responsibilities for one of our senior staff members," says Kathleen Buescher. "That was a big mistake. It set her and us up for failure. As soon as things started popping, it pulled her away. We should have taken the time early on to find a full-time CEO whose sole interest and total energies could go to developing the company."

  - *Inadequate compensation:* One of the most severe shocks to the system of an established NGO is discovering how expensive talent can be. The CEO of a social sector business owned by an NGO will frequently earn (or have the opportunity to earn) a much higher salary than the CEO of the parent organization. It takes a courageous parent CEO to let that happen.

  - *Inadequate flexibility:* Few things will de-motivate an entrepreneur more than having to carry out somebody else's business plan. "Don't be afraid to hire somebody smarter than you – then give them the freedom to operate!" says Jim Westall, whose business in Port Townsend, Washington, takes young men off welfare. "Use benchmarks to monitor their work – *but get out of their way!*" In other words, find a CEO first, then let him or her create the business plan.

- *The senior management team:* One of the findings during the ten-year MIT study of 814,000 small businesses during the 1980s and 1990s was this: The survival rate of companies that had at least five people in the brain trust at the beginning was substantially higher than those that had four or fewer.[23] The first thing smart CEOs do is surround themselves with people who have the talents and expertise they lack.

- *Industry expertise:* "It's relatively easy to enter the temporary help business," says Roy Soards, who did it successfully in Oregon. "There aren't many obstacles. But our biggest mistake was not bringing in an expert from the start. We thought this would be a really easy business, and we simply didn't get the expertise we needed. We don't do this anymore. Any time we start a new business these days we hire expertise first." Julius Walls of Greyston Bakery could not agree more emphatically. "It may sound obvious," he says, "but it needs to be emphasized. We needed to have expertise in bakery science. We understood the *art*, but we didn't understand the *science*, how ingredients react with each other and why. We understood how to make our product every day, yes, but if somebody asked us to deviate from what we were doing it wasn't as clear how to change and modify." And when Bobbie Lenz started searching for somebody to run her bulk mailing business in Duluth, Minnesota, that employs people who are developmentally disabled, she turned to a woman who had significant experience working for the post office. "It made a very big difference," says Lenz. "No matter what kind of business you start, you have to be an expert at what you're doing. If you don't do that, you don't have anything to offer. With us, it meant we had to learn the mailing regulations and keep up with constant changes – so our customers wouldn't have to." Kathleen Buescher emphasizes that at least some of the Board members for any social sector business should also have experience in the specific industry – not doing so hampered her initial efforts in St. Louis. And a thriving direct mail catalog business for women operated by a women's shelter in New York state failed because when times got tough (paper costs, fulfillment costs and online competition all escalating), there was nobody on the Board who understood the nuts and bolts of the business well enough to be helpful.

- *The employees:* Building an effective group of employees – and a viable social sector business – requires NGOs to meet at least three basic challenges:

  - *Recruiting and retaining people with the right attitudes and skills:* NGOs installing an entrepreneurial culture will often have to make some tough choices about staff members. Some of their most loyal, long-term employees will not understand the new culture. Some who do will not accept it. And some of those who embrace it will not have the talents to thrive. Some form of compassionate out-placement is the best solution, for them and for the organization.

- *Creating a blended workforce:* Most social sector businesses that employ the people they serve develop what is known as a blended workforce. The optimum mix differs depending on the type of business, but 60 to 75 per cent of the employees are typically drawn from the target population, the rest from the general population.

- *Firing people who do not perform:* Rick Walker's businesses employ people who are developmentally disabled, but he says "you've got to be absolutely ruthless about making changes whenever they're needed. We fire people." Julius Walls is equally adamant. "We do *not* do make-work," he says. "We don't have pseudo-welfare jobs or a sheltered workshop. You *must* perform. We have very strict standards." John DuRand, the retired founder of Minnesota Diversified Industries, calls it "giving people the dignity of allowing them the opportunity to fail," and Jim Westall says "there *is* a lot of dignity in knowing what the expectations are and being able to achieve them, being in a workplace where you really feel valued. We benchmark everything, so people know how they contribute to the success of the company. That's tremendously important for them, to know they're part of something significant."

7. The separation strategy

In Paul Firstenberg's book *Managing for Profit in the Nonprofit World*, he writes:

> The basic point . . . is that the creation of a successful profit-making component within a not-for-profit environment – the building of a culture-within-a-culture, so to speak – is a difficult business . . . . The chances of successfully doing so will be enhanced if the (profit-making) component is, from the outset, clearly labeled as such, and its different objectives and need for a different operating style are recognized from the start. . . . The greater the separation in terms of form, staffing, oversight, and location, the greater are the chances that the profit-making component will be able to function with the necessary clarity of purpose and operating style appropriate to its objectives.[24]

Entrepreneurial business ventures have to move quickly, and they cannot do so if they are encumbered by bureaucracy. For that reason, any social sector business started by an NGO should be kept as separate as possible from the parent organization's other operations. Furthermore, although it is reasonable to incubate the business internally for a short period of time, the sooner and more completely it can be separated, the better its chances for success.

Part of the separation strategy for a social sector business is a willingness to create an independent Board of Directors, which should have no more than six or seven members, most of them outsiders:

- Three or four should be proven entrepreneurs

- One should be a person in the business of starting businesses (a seed capitalist or an attorney specializing in startups)
- One should be the senior executive of the parent NGO (to serve as the conscience of the new company, but not to become involved in operations)
- One should be a champion from the parent Board who is specifically charged with protecting the new venture from interference by either the parent Board or staff

Relinquishing control of day-to-day operations in a social sector business is a terribly difficult thing for most NGO Board and staff members to do, but, as Firstenberg points out, it is a fundamentally important strategy, especially when taking a business to scale.

8. Strategic marketing

Marketing is *not* a business function – it *is* the business. And it begins when the senior management team makes two important strategic decisions: What products or services to offer and what target markets to pursue.

Unfortunately, when most social entrepreneurs begin thinking about marketing, they immediately focus on tactics: Creating a brochure, writing a news release, staging a special event, offering a discount. Strategic and tactical marketing are certainly related, but strategic marketing is the parent and tactical marketing the child.

The key *strategic* marketing questions are these:

- Who are our customers?
- What do they want/need/value?
- Can *we* provide it?
- *Should* we provide it?
- How should we position ourselves?
- Can we win?

The key *tactical* marketing weapons are these:

- Packaging (product or service design)
- Pricing
- Distribution channels
- Marketing communications (advertising, publicity, sales promotion, personal selling)

There are two fundamental marketing strategies, both of which are relevant for social entrepreneurs:

- *Market push:* This is the only strategy available when a social entrepreneur is attempting to introduce a product or service that has never before been commercialized (for example, hospice care in the United States in the 1970s) – the entrepreneur must "push" the new product or service into the market (a process sometimes called "market development'). It is a long and difficult journey.

- *Market pull:* The situation is different when an NGO is thinking about entering a market already occupied by competitors, which is typically what happens when an established NGO attempts to capitalize on its organizational strengths by starting a business. The temptation is to push – to start with its established products and services, offer them for sale and hope somebody will buy them – but the proper approach is to *start with potential customers, discover what they need, then build it.* In this way the NGO will be *pulled* into the market by its customers, a vastly preferable situation.

9. Viability first, not mission

Perhaps the greatest obstacle Jim Westall sees in running a social sector business is what he calls "value rubs." Sometimes, he says, "you have to make decisions about sustainability that are at least temporarily in conflict with your mission. You just *have* to do it. You have to depersonalize those conflicts and solve the problem. But in my work with other nonprofits, I've seen those value rubs absolutely destroy their businesses."

Implicit in the argument offered by Westall and others is the belief that if the business is not viable, it will not survive – and, if it fails, the entire discussion about social impact becomes irrelevant. Dale Novotny of Applied Industries in Longview, Washington, who provides employment opportunities for people who are disabled, makes the point succinctly: "We've always been very focused on being a business first. We're a social service business second."

Rich Gilmartin ran into a "value rub" in his Florida janitorial business, which employs people who are developmentally disabled. "In order to keep our prices competitive," he says, "we're consistently looking for ways to introduce new technology, and that usually translates into automation or more efficient equipment. For example, we've traditionally had a person manually operating a floor-waxing machine that can do swipes of 24 to 28 inches wide. But now we've identified some labor-saving machinery that's much more expensive on the initial end but will reduce our labor consumption and allow us to hold down costs. That means we'll be employing fewer people in the short run, but in the long run it can make our prices competitive and allow us to secure more contracts – and ultimately create even more jobs."

10. Focus, focus, focus

Over the years, social entrepreneurs have learned some painful lessons about the market. Here are three:

- *Do not wander too far afield:* Too many NGOs are charmed by the promise of an unrelated business, a cash cow that somehow supports its social mission. During the late 1970s and again during the early 1980s, a number of nonprofits across the United States began to pursue unrelated business income in an attempt to offset the escalating cuts in federal and state funding. However, this meant they were delving into areas unrelated to their social mission, and most of the efforts failed: The nonprofits were not only trying to start a business (which they did not know how to do), but were also trying to do it in an arena they knew nothing about.

- *Find and define a niche:* The market can be tumultuous and cruel. To succeed, social entrepreneurs must have a sound business concept, regardless of whether they are enhancing an internal program or contemplating a spin-off business venture. In other words, they need a market *niche* – a product or service, somebody who wants it, and somebody who is willing and able to pay for it. For NGOs, of course, the last part is frequently the toughest, because the "client" and the "customer" are often two different parties. But, as Paul Hawken says in his book, *Growing a Business*, the goal of any entrepreneurial effort is to reduce the business idea to its essence – and then continue reducing it until reaching a space that is small enough to defend but large enough to achieve the organization's financial objectives.[25]

- *Be a player or do not play at all:* This one takes real courage, but it gives NGOs a way to grapple with the classic "80/20" problem that occurs when they devote 80 per cent of their management time trying to fix the 20 per cent of their programs that should actually be eliminated. It is very difficult for NGOs to kill programs, but the pain can often be mitigated by finding a home for them in another organization better positioned to provide the service. By doing so, NGOs will simultaneously be freeing themselves to concentrate on the programs where *they* are better positioned – and the clients and customers of *both* NGOs will be better served.

11. Customer service

The customer may not always be right, but the customer is *always* the customer. Once a social enterprise is underway, customer service is the most important factor for ongoing success.

For example, one of the biggest surprises for Kathleen Buescher has been discovering that "when you're working with the corporate sector, *everything* is negotiable, unlike government contracts where it's 'thou shalt and thou shalt not.' So it's very important to stay in tune with your corporate customers, stay very attentive and sensitive to their needs. We don't want to be just a short-term contractor. We want to be an ongoing resource to supervisors and to management."

"We will never forget our customers are the ones who keep us in business," says Kevin McDonald, "so you have to treat 'em right. They are *always* right. If we do something wrong, we respond immediately and take care of the problem. That's just *so* important . . .but people forget that. When customers appreciate what you've done it's the best form of advertising you can get. It's like buying cars: You go back to somebody you're comfortable with."

Almost by accident, Bobbie Lenz discovered customer service gave her company a unique selling proposition. "Right from the beginning," she says, "as a nonprofit, we were always mission driven, always centered on what was best for our clients. But very early in our existence as a business we realized running it successfully meant we had to use the *same* approach with customers. 'Here we are,' we said. 'What do you need? We'll do *everything* to meet your needs.'" That determination to do what was best for its clients *and* for its customers emerged from what Lenz calls one of her organization's core values: The importance of choice for people who are developmentally disabled. "That's what our business venture has been all about," she says. "These days, customer service is hard to find, but we've bent over *backwards* to provide *extraordinary* customer service. We're definitely people-oriented, and that's part of our heritage as a nonprofit." She also discovered a practical reason to emphasize customer service. "Initially," she says, "here we were, this human service agency with severely disabled people doing mailings, and a lot of people had a problem with that. So we never used the heart on the sleeve, 'Oh, please put these poor people to work,' approach. Right from the beginning we said, 'Use us. You need to. It's good business.' That's why referrals and word of mouth have worked so well for us. You need to act like a business, not a human service agency."

Rich Gilmartin predicts "if we're not accessible to the customer, we probably won't be their vendor very long. Customers often tell us management for previous vendors stayed at a great distance, never came to talk with them – and if decisions had to be made, the local person was not empowered to make them. So we mount a concerted effort to empower the person on the site to make the greatest scope of decisions possible – and we also have people from our headquarters office traveling to each site on a regular basis, in part to spot problems before the customer sees them and they become big problems."

One of the obstacles Gilmartin and his staff have managed to overcome has been "not hearing a message early enough." As an example, he cites the company's custodial contract on a naval air base. "They'd been telling us for months we were missing the mark," he remembers. "They weren't ringing any fire alarms or loud bells, but they were saying improvements were needed here and there. We were listening – we thought – but then we discounted the information and came up with reasons why things were the way they were and why we were doing everything we could be doing. Then they set off the fire alarm. 'We've been telling you for six months that things need to be fixed,' they said, 'and we've seen no noticeable attempt to fix them. So now your contract's at risk.' It took us 18 months to eradicate that situation and turn it around. It didn't take that long to fix the problems, but it did take that long for the base to believe our fix would stick."

Gilmartin also believes his company takes customer service a lot farther than most. "If you just do what people expect, and that's it," he says, "they almost don't know you're there – and when it comes time for contract renewal or adding contracts there's no substantial advantage. On the other hand, it makes a difference if you do something a little out of the ordinary – like leave behind your business card with a handwritten note, or leave a Hershey's candy kiss on someone's desk, or if you find a $5 bill on the floor and call it to the attention of the ownership instead of shoving it into your pocket and walking away. It can be any number of things," he says. In many situations, for example, the previous vendor did not wear uniforms. Gulf Coast employees not only wear uniforms, "but we put our name on them and we let customers pick the color. It all sets a tone immediately that is different than what the customers expect."

12. Quality

"We will make no compromises on quality just because the work has been done by people with disabilities," says Rick Walker. "If you rent a room at our motel it will be the bloody cleanest hotel you've ever been in. If you go into our ice cream store you'll have a perfect experience. Not, 'Isn't that cute!' but 'This is great!' I make life miserable for people around me on that issue." Walker says community skepticism about the ability of his organization to successfully operate its businesses "can only be overcome in two ways. Number one, don't give them an avenue for an opening by having quality failures. And the other is to outlive the bastards and patiently go about what you've been doing."

"The customer won't pay for mistakes," says Bobbie Lenz. "If you screw up, you're costing yourself money, so quality control is essential. You have to do it right the first time."

And Rich Gilmartin believes measuring employee performance is critical. "Before we started actually doing it," he says, "we would sometimes say 'this is important' and then not measure it, or we'd measure it for a time and stop – and lo and behold performance would deteriorate. So now we do focus groups and have periodic performance meetings with our clients. We track things historically to see if they're on the rise, or flat – or, worse yet, going downward."

What sets Jim Westall's asbestos abatement company aside from its eight competitors in the state of Washington is its certification as an ISO 14000 provider, an international environmental quality standard. "You have to be able to document precisely what's happening with the asbestos every step of the way," he says, "so it can be tracked for at least 20 years. Sometimes we can't remove it, so our job is simply to encase it so it can't be touched." Being certified gives Skookum an edge on its competitors and also reassures its clients. "Here we are," laughs Westall, "telling our customers we'll do asbestos abatement – and that we're going to hire the least capable members of the community to do it! In an area that has a tremendous liability for the customer! And they're going to look at us and say, 'Huh, sure you are!' And we can say we're the only asbestos abatement company in the state of Washington that is ISO certified."

13. Aggressive pricing

When setting pricing strategies, NGOs are gradually learning to think in terms of annual budgets, not just unit costs. For example, successful for-profit service companies in the United States typically have a *gross* profit margin of 40 to 60 percent on everything they sell – in order to finish the year with an over-all *net* margin (after overhead, payroll and other internal and external sales costs have been deducted) of three to five percent.[26] In other words, if it costs $1.00 to deliver a product or service, NGOs need to be charging $1.40 to $1.60.

Of course, abruptly introducing price hikes of that magnitude would come as a shock to most current payers. Nevertheless, any NGO hoping to become increasingly sustainable or self-sufficient will have to consider this approach and, at the very least, begin raising its prices incrementally. Rich Gilmartin's company frequently wins contracts despite having a *higher* price than its competitors. "Often," he says, "the customers have already been there – and realize they may have shot themselves in the foot by going with the lower price. Now they're looking around because they feel like they're not getting what they expected – or maybe they're just asking for a higher level of service."

However, charging a price is one thing, collecting another. Dave McDonough discovered a harsh truth: "You pay your employees every Friday and you send out invoices once a week," he says, "but you don't get paid for 30 or 45 days." At one point during its history, his Los Angeles social enterprise "had a bad accounts receivable problem, and we discovered the primary reason was our inability to get our invoices out on time. And then when they *did* go out they were wrong! So the customer would say, 'Well, this one's wrong, I'll just set it over here.' It was amazing, really. So we hired a woman for our finance department who had a background in collections – and it turned out it wasn't really a collections issue at all as much as it was a follow-up issue. After that we made sure the invoices went out on time, called customers to follow up and in just a few months went from having about 60 per cent of our accounts receivable unpaid after 90 days to having the bulk of them paid within 45 days."

One of the major pressures on pricing, of course, is competition, which often changes the landscape dramatically. "There used to be more companies competing with us," says Kathleen Buescher. "Now there are fewer, they're a lot bigger, and they've turned employee counseling into a commodity business. And that means pricing has become a very big deal. We used to be able to charge our corporate customers $30 or $35 per year per employee – now it's down to $12 to $18."

14. Strategic partnerships

Few businesses today can survive in the market without forging strategic partnerships. Four of the most powerful types include operational philanthropy[27], supplier relationships, distributor relationships, and cause-related marketing ("licensing").

- *Operational philanthropy* occurs when a for-profit company creates a business relationship with a nonprofit instead of giving it a grant – *and therefore becomes dependent on the nonprofit's performance for its own success.* For example, Pioneer Human Services in Seattle, Washington, employs disadvantaged men and women to manufacture aerospace and sheet metal products for the aircraft, telecommunications, electronic and other industries (including cargo liners and more than 8,000 other parts for Boeing aircraft). Pioneer businesses also include warehousing, assembly, contract packaging and food purchasing services, plus a central kitchen facility and a number of retail cafes, and the total annual revenue from all of them in 2004 came to more than $51 million – with 99.7 per cent coming from earned income. The company, led by President Mike Burns, recently received national recognition for "pioneering a new model for social change and setting an agenda for nonprofit organizations nationwide."[28]

- A *supplier relationship* takes place when either the NGO or the for-profit company supplies personnel, raw materials and/or finished components to the other. Greyston Bakery is a prime example: It supplies more than 10,000 pounds of brownies and blondies a day – nearly three million pounds a year – that are used in five Ben & Jerry's ice cream products in the United States and in its products throughout Europe and the Mideast. Annual sales for Greyston are $4.2 million, with a 3.7 per cent net profit – and the bakery provides 50 jobs for ex-convicts and others who have barriers to employment.

- *A distributor relationship* occurs when either a for-profit company or an NGO channels its products or services to customers through the other organization's network. A common example in the United States takes place when for-profit companies partner with nonprofits to access federal and state "set-aside" programs (in which government contracts are offered first to nonprofits). Another is the relationship Bobbie Lenz's bulk mailing business has with the post office. "They've given us a lot of technical assistance and taught us everything we've learned about the business," she says, "and, for them, having an organization like us is helpful, because it reduces the number of organizations showing up with bulk mailings that aren't sorted or otherwise ready for mailing. When people like that come to them, the post office sends them to us."

- *Cause-related marketing* occurs when a nonprofit licenses the use of its name to a commercial company. The combination can be powerful: It can enhance the reputation and boost the sales of a for-profit company and simultaneously increase the credibility and generate earned income for a nonprofit. For example, during 90-day periods in the spring of five consecutive years, each person who used an American Express credit card in the United States knew four per cent of his or her purchase price went directly to Share Our Strength, one of the nation's leading anti-hunger organizations. The partnership raised $43 million and funded more than 1,000 local, state, national and international organizations. But the goals do not have to be so ambitious: When Clif Bar, Inc., one of the country's leading manufacturers of energy bars, decided to help the Breast Cancer Foundation by creating the LunaBar and donating a percentage of sales to the Foundation, the first year's proceeds were only $5,000 – but by 2004 had grown to more than $300,000 per year, about 10 per cent of the Foundation's annual operating budget.

Conclusion

The rules of the game for NGOs have changed dramatically during the past 20 years. Operating costs have soared, resources available from traditional sources have flattened, the ranks of NGOs competing for grants and subsidies have mushroomed, and the number of people in need has escalated beyond our most troubling nightmares.

This essay has been an attempt to clarify both the promise and the perils attached to social entrepreneurship. And the pioneers in the field have some final warnings:

- *Do not enter the world of entrepreneurship unless you are personally energized by the idea – it is not for the faint of heart.* Do not attempt to do it because you think you "should" or because others insist. Unless you are ignited by the prospect, unless it drives you out of bed in the morning and sends you charging into the day, it is not for you.

- *Ask yourselves some important threshold questions.* Is this something we *really* want to do? Is the timing right? Do we understand the risks and are we willing to take them? Are we being realistic about possible results? Do we have enough staying power (money, time, psychic energy)? Have we the right people – and are we willing to give them the freedom, responsibility and authority necessary for entrepreneurial success? Positive answers to these and other questions will not guarantee success, but they may give you the confidence to proceed.

- *Do not underestimate the resources you will need:* The biggest mistake Jim Westall made when developing his asbestos abatement business "was the timeline. We thought it wouldn't take nearly the capital or the time. You know, the old 'rosy scenario' planning process. We kept digging into our capital." And the necessary resources were not limited to money: They also included people, facilities, time and other scarce commodities. "In order to get started," says Westall, "we had to acquire a whole different level of skills. We really had to gear up. We had to train ourselves and then our employees. It took months and months of pretty intensive work, and we climbed into a large hole before we got out with our first contract. We spent almost half a million dollars buying equipment, traveling, buying people, getting people trained. But we were in it for the long haul."

- *Watch the numbers, every day:* It became apparent to Tony Wagner early on that his training as a nonprofit manager did not prepare him for the realities of running a business. "You've got to have an absolutely brutal discipline about the financial end of the business," he says. "I'd been a nonprofit manager for years, but until we started our business there'd never been a time when I needed *daily* financial information."

- *Grow organically.* The most dangerous time for any small business is when it attempts to grow from being a "big small" business into a "small big" business. Financial resources are stretched, emotional stress escalates, psychic energy dissipates, competitors get in the way. "We made some significant mistakes," admits Rich Gilmartin. "We were still operating as though we were a twenty-five to a hundred person operation long after we'd passed that point." Dave McDonough remembers "the vacuum effect" when a large customer "sucked up people from everywhere and became our only focus. It was a shock to the system." And Richard Oulahan emphasizes how important it is for NGOs to sometimes say no, either because it rubs against their mission or because it dangerously extends their resources.

- *Be flexible.* There are no guarantees, no perfect plans. All the other advice offered by the pioneers in the field is simply a way to shape the field of play: Ultimately, success or failure depends on the willingness of social entrepreneurs to do whatever is necessary. As a wise man once said, "Things turn out best for those who make the best of the way things turn out."[29]

Making the transition from innovation to entrepreneurship is fraught with dangers. Years ago, Pablo Eisenberg, Founder and Chairman Emeritus of the National Committee for Responsive Philanthropy, wrote that "far too many charities have . . . forgotten the distinction between for-profit and non-profit activities, between fulfilling a mission and survival at any cost. . . . The appeal of non-profit organizations is their commitment to public service . . . it is not as a shadow private sector."[30] But, according to Kenneth Mason, the former Chairman of Quaker Oats, "making a profit is no more the purpose of a corporation than getting enough to eat is the purpose of life. Getting enough to eat is a *requirement* of life. Life's purpose, one would hope, is something broader and more challenging. Likewise with business and profit."[31]

And nonprofit executive Robert Harrington may have put it most succinctly, and in terms social entrepreneurs would resoundingly endorse: "If you want to help the poor people of the world," he said, "step one is to make sure you're not one of them!"

Notes

1. Bailey, Anne Lowrey, "1980's Giving Boom Not Matched by Growth for Many Groups," *The Chronicle of Philanthropy*, January 9, 1990, 4.
2. *Ibid*, 4.
3. Williams, Grant, "Generosity of Wealthy Donors Dropped in 1980's, but Overall Giving Held Steady, Study Finds," *The Chronicle of Philanthropy*, June 2, 1992, 17.
4. Kaplan, Ann E. (ed.), *Giving USA 1995: The Annual Report on Philanthropy for the Year 1994* (New York, New York: AAFRC Trust for Philanthropy, 1995), 77.
5. Hodgkinson, Virginia Ann, Murray S. Weitzman, Christopher M. Toppe and Stephen M. Noga, *Nonprofit Almanac 1992-1993: Dimensions of the Independent Sector* (San Francisco, California: Jossey-Bass Publishers, 1992), 59.
6. Weitzman, Murray S., Nadine T. Jalandoni, Linda M. Lampkin and Thomas H. Pollak, *The New Nonprofit Almanac and Desk Reference: The Essential Facts and Figures for Managers, Researchers, and Volunteers* (New York, New York: Jossey-Bass, A Wiley Company, 2002), 57.
7. *Ibid*, 5.
8. Berg, Steve, "36,900,000: Americans in Poverty in "92," *Star Tribune*, October 5, 1993, 2A.
9. *Ibid*, 4A.
10. "Working Poor Grow in Number: 1 in 5 full-time employees now counted in category, study says," *Star Tribune*, October 7, 1993.
11. "Social Services Gap," *NonProfit Times*, February 1993, 57.
12. Toppe, Christopher and Arthur D. Kirsch, *Keeping the Trust: Confidence in Charitable Organizations in an Age of Scrutiny* (Washington, D.C.: Independent Sector, August 2002), 2.
13. Much of the material in this section has been developed jointly with Jim McClurg, Vice President of The Social Enterprise Alliance, the leading membership organization for social entrepreneurs in the United States. McClurg previously served for 25 years as CEO of Northwest Center Industries in Seattle, Washington, one of the nation's most successful social enterprises. During his tenure, he developed a network of small businesses that generated more than $15 million in annual sales, employed 400 adults with disabilities and reduced grant income to less than 3% of budgeted expenses.

14. *Webster's New World Dictionary*, 1982 ed.

15. Brodsky, Norm, "Who Are the Real Entrepreneurs?," *Inc.*, December 1996, 33.

16. Dees, J. Gregory, Jed Emerson and Peter Economy, *Enterprising Nonprofits: A Toolkit for Social Entrepreneurs* (New York, New York: John Wiley & Sons, Inc., 2001), 5.

17. Sterne, Larry, "Management Guru Calls on Nonprofits," *The NonProfit Times*, May, 1989, 10-11, 37-38.

18. Remarks by Charles King, Chair, Board of Directors, The National Gathering for Social Entrepreneurs, at The 4th National Gathering for Social Entrepreneurs, Minneapolis, Minnesota, December 4-6, 2002.

19. Maxwell, John C., *Failing Forward: Turning Mistakes into Stepping-Stones for Success* (Nashville, Tennessee: Thomas Nelson Publishers, 2000), 47-48.

20. Barker, Joel Arthur, *Discovering the Future Series: The Business of Paradigms* (Burnsville, Minnesota: Charthouse Learning, 1989), on page 26 of the printed materials accompanying the video.

21. Kirchoff, Bruce A., "Entrepreneurship Economics," *The Portable MBA in Entrepreneurship*, 2nd ed. (New York, New York: John Wiley & Sons, Inc., 1997), 461.

22. "Business Success and Failure," *MEC: The Minnesota Entrepreneurs" Club* newsletter, date unknown, 1.

23. Kirchoff, Bruce A., "Entrepreneurship Economics," *The Portable MBA in Entrepreneurship*, 2nd edn. (New York, New York: John Wiley & Sons, Inc., 1997), 461.

24. Firstenberg, Paul B., *Managing for Profit in the Nonprofit World* (New York, New York: The Foundation Center, 1986), 63-64.

25. Hawken, Paul, *Growing a Business* (New York, New York: Simon & Schuster, 1987).

26. Timmons, Jeffry A., "Opportunity Recognition: The Search for Higher-Potential Ventures," *The Portable MBA in Entrepreneurship* (New York, New York: John Wiley & Sons, Inc., 1994), 26.

27. Gary Mulhair created the phrase "operational philanthropy" in 1997 during his tenure as President and CEO of Pioneer Human Services, Seattle, Washington.

28. Dahle, Cheryl, "Social Justice – Pioneer Human Services," *Fast Company*, April 2000, 172.

29. Attributed to former United States Vice President Hubert H. Humphrey.

30. Eisenberg, Pablo, "Corporate Values Could Poison Nonprofits," *The Chronicle of Philanthropy*, March 10, 1992.

31. Makower, J., *Beyond the Bottom Line* (New York, New York: Simon & Schuster, 1994), 31-32.

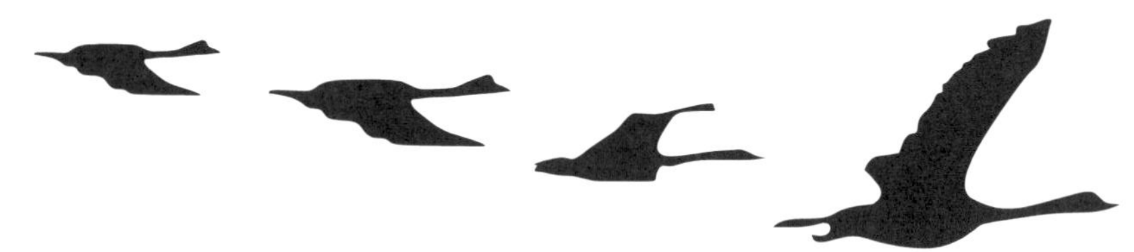

SECTION TWO

A practical lexicon for social entrepreneurs

A Practical Lexicon for Social Entrepreneurs

Words or phrases appearing in boldface italics are defined elsewhere in the lexicon

AFFIRMATIVE BUSINESS: A ***social enterprise*** created specifically to provide permanent jobs, competitive wages, career tracks and ownership opportunities for people who are disadvantaged, whether it be mentally, physically, economically or educationally. John DuRand of Minnesota Diversified Industries created the concept in 1973 and simultaneously emphasized the importance of a ***blended work force***. The employees for an affirmative business might include people who are developmentally disabled, chronically mentally ill, recovering substance abusers, former convicts, visually impaired, physically challenged, or grappling with some other disadvantage. In the United Kingdom, an affirmative business is known as a "social firm."

BLENDED VALUE: While every organization attempts to create value of one kind or another, the central premise of the blended value proposition is that value is itself a combination, a "blend," of economic, environmental and social factors, and that maximizing value requires taking all three elements into account, regardless of whether the organization is in the for-profit or nonprofit sector. The key areas in which both investors and organizations are working to maximize the impact of blended value are ***corporate social responsibility, social enterprise, social investing, strategic***

philanthropy and ***sustainable development***. Jed Emerson and Sheila Bonini began developing the concept of blended value in 2003.

BLENDED WORK FORCE: In order to maximize productivity and increase its ability to compete, an ***affirmative business*** commonly employs a blended work force comprised of people who are mentally, physically, economically or educationally disadvantaged and those who are not. A typical mix draws about 60 to 75 per cent of the employees from the ranks of people who are disadvantaged.

BUSINESS MENTORS: Among others, the ***entrepreneurial planning team*** assembled to help create a ***social sector business*** typically includes three or four entrepreneurs who have built successful businesses from the ground up. These veteran entrepreneurs provide an invaluable reality check throughout the planning process.

BUSINESS PLAN: The essential ingredients of a business plan include an executive summary (typically written last); descriptions of the company, the management team, and the products or services being offered; an analysis of the market, the competition and the industry (including ***critical success factors*** and ***environmental forces***); a ***marketing plan***; an operations plan; a financial plan (with cash flow projections); and a ***risk analysis*** (the most important part of the plan). Most effective business plans contain no more than 20 to 30 pages of narrative plus financials.

BUYER: The ***customer*** and the ***client*** are not always the same, but both are buyers. Customers are those who *pay* for a product or service: They are interested in both the price and the social outcomes. Clients are those who *receive* a product or service: They are interested *primarily* in the social outcomes.

CAUSE-RELATED MARKETING: Cause-related marketing occurs when a nonprofit licenses the use of its name to a commercial company. The combination can be powerful: It can enhance the reputation and boost the sales of the commercial company and simultaneously expand the reach and generate ***earned income*** for the nonprofit. Cause-related marketing is one of the four most effective types of strategic partnerships between a commercial company and a nonprofit. See ***distributor relationships, operational philanthropy*** and ***supplier relationships***.

CAUSE-RELATED PURCHASING: A business relationship in which a commercial company, as part of its ongoing business operations, purchases components or finished piecework provided by a nonprofit. Dan McKinnon coined the phrase in 1998 during his tenure as President and CEO of NISH, formerly known as National Industries for the Severely Handicapped. See ***operational philanthropy***.

CLIENT: The individual or the organization receiving a product or service. If the client is not the ***customer***, he or she will be interested *primarily* in the social outcomes, not the price.

CORE VALUES: A set of fundamental beliefs that define an organization and dictate the behavior of its employees. To be effective, core values must be clearly articulated, institutionalized, and constantly reinforced: Organizations should identify them before doing anything else; make sure they can be quantified; build them into strategic plans and annual operating plans; monitor them religiously; measure progress periodically; and report results to ***stakeholders***. To qualify as a "core" value, an organization must be willing to live with the consequences of embracing it, the value must be freely chosen from genuine alternatives, it must be acted upon as a regular pattern of action, it must apply everywhere in the work, it must last over time, and the organization must be proud of it.

CORPORATE SOCIAL RESPONSIBILITY (CSR): The CSR movement calls for businesses to behave ethically and contribute to economic development while improving the quality of life for employees, local communities and society at large. A socially responsible company will identify and engage its ***stakeholders***, then determine, measure and report the ways in which they are affected.

CRITICAL SUCCESS FACTORS: Beyond the factors that must exist for *any* business to succeed (*e.g.,* capable management, positive cash flow), there are also critical factors that differ depending upon the *type* of business (*e.g.,* location, price, distribution, convenience, options, warranties). Unless entrepreneurs can identify the factors that apply to *their* type of business and compete effectively in those areas, they will fail.

CUSTOMER: The individual or the organization purchasing a product or service. The customer may or may not be the ***client***. As ***buyers***, customers are interested in both the price and the social outcomes.

DEPENDENCY: The traditional business model for nonprofits, in which they depend solely or almost entirely on charitable contributions and ***public sector subsidies***, with ***earned income*** either non-existent or minimal. See ***sustainability*** and ***self-sufficiency***.

DIRECT COSTS: The actual, out-of-pocket expenses associated with a program, product, service or business (*e.g.*, travel expenses, long-distance telephone charges, conference fees). See also ***indirect costs***.

DISTRIBUTION CHANNELS: One of the four parts of the ***marketing mix***. Distribution channels are the routes products and services travel from the provider to the receiver. There may be intermediaries along the way (individuals or institutions) that must be compensated as part of a company's distribution costs.

DISTRIBUTOR RELATIONSHIPS: Distributor relationships occur when either a commercial company or a nonprofit channels its products or services to customers through the other's network. A common example in the United States takes place when commercial companies partner with nonprofits to access federal and state "set-aside" programs (in which government contracts are offered first to nonprofits). Distributor relationships are one of the four most powerful types of strategic partnerships between a commercial company and a nonprofit. See ***cause-related marketing, operational philanthropy*** and ***supplier relationships***.

DOUBLE BOTTOM LINE: The simultaneous pursuit of financial and social ***returns on investment*** – the ultimate benchmark for a ***social enterprise*** or a ***social sector business***. See ***triple bottom line***.

DUE DILIGENCE: The process potential investors use to investigate and evaluate a business venture before committing funds. Due diligence also can refer to the process used by a ***social enterprise*** to assess the viability of ideas for ***earned income strategies*** or a ***social sector business***. See ***market research*** and ***feasibility studies***.

EARNED INCOME: Income is "earned" when there is a *quid pro quo* – a direct exchange of product, service or privilege for monetary value. Earned income for a nonprofit includes such things as tuition payments, the sale of products or services, government contracts, consulting fees, membership dues (when dues purchase tangible benefits), sale of intellectual property, agreement to use the nonprofit's identity, royalties, ticket sales, property rentals/leases, and so on. Earned income does *not* include such things as corporate or foundation grants, government grants or subsidies, financial contributions from individuals, or in-kind donation of products or services. Most ***earned income strategies*** mounted by a nonprofit are designed to cover part of a specific program's cost, not necessarily make a profit; the program makes up the difference through charitable contributions and ***public sector subsidies***. The one exception is a ***social sector business***, which depends on earned income alone.

EARNED INCOME STRATEGIES: An attempt by a nonprofit to cover part of its costs by capitalizing on the ***earned income*** potential of its programs, products and services. A strategy that depends *entirely* on earned income is called a ***social sector business***.

ENGAGED PHILANTHROPY: See ***venture philanthropy***.

ENTREPRENEUR: A person who organizes and manages a business undertaking, assuming the risk for the sake of profit. Starting with nothing more than an idea or a prototype, entrepreneurs have the ability to take a business to the point at which it can sustain itself on internally generated cash flow. Generally speaking, entrepreneurs need the freedom to operate without much supervision. They also need clear definitions of success and failure, *immediate* feedback, rewards for performance, and ongoing challenges. See ***social entrepreneur, nonprofit entrepreneur*** and ***entrepreneurial nonprofit***.

ENTREPRENEURIAL BRAINSTORMING: A facilitated process designed to generate ideas for ***earned income strategies*** or a ***social sector business***. An effective process typically lasts no more than 90 minutes and involves about 20 people. To make sure all possible ideas are broached, every idea is welcomed, criticisms are not allowed, and nobody is held accountable for his or her idea. The ideas generated during an entrepreneurial brainstorming session fall into one of four categories: *Market penetration* (offering an existing product or service to an existing ***target market***); *market development* (offering an existing product or service to a new target market); p*roduct or service development* (offering a new product or service to an existing target market); or *diversification* (offering a new product or service to a new target market).

ENTREPRENEURSHIP: The ability to convert an idea or a prototype into a business that can sustain itself on internally generated cash flow. See ***innovation***.

ENTREPRENEURIAL NONPROFIT: A nonprofit that seeks to match its core competencies with marketplace opportunities in order to simultaneously generate more ***earned income*** and expand its social impact.

ENTREPRENEURIAL PLANNING TEAM: A group of experts assembled by a nonprofit when it begins planning a ***social sector business***. In addition to members of senior management, a typical team might include three or four members of the Board of

Directors; three or four ***business mentors*** (successful entrepreneurs from the local community); and at least one or two *wild cards*, people who know very little about the organization but will act as devil's advocates throughout the planning process.

ENTREPRENEURIAL STRATEGIC PLANNING (ESP): A process by which a ***social enterprise*** analyzes each of its products and services from both a social impact and an ***earned income*** perspective. The goal is to create an entrepreneurial ***business plan*** that expands the organization's most effective and needed products and services and productively disposes of its more peripheral ones (see ***organized abandonment***). Making these types of strategic decisions, however, is more difficult for a social enterprise than it is for either a traditional nonprofit or a purely commercial company, both of which are primarily concerned with a single bottom line. A traditional nonprofit will continue offering products and services that have a significant social impact even if they lose money; commercial companies will not. On the other hand, a social enterprise will give weight to *both* bottom lines before making decisions about which products and services to expand, nurture, harvest or kill. The intersection of social impact and financial returns can be viewed as a matrix:

	Positive financial returns	*Negative financial returns*
Significant social impact	EXPAND	NURTURE
Minimal social impact	HARVEST	KILL

ENTRY STRATEGY: A nonprofit starting a ***social sector business***

will either deliver a product or service that is already being offered by others or create one that has never been offered before. In either case, it will typically enter the market by developing the business itself, buying a franchise, purchasing an existing company, or forging a ***strategic partnership***. See ***feasibility studies*** and ***market research***.

ENVIRONMENTAL FORCES: The uncontrollable forces (demographic, economic, sociological, technological, political and regulatory) that have a positive or negative effect on an ***earned income strategy*** or a ***social sector business***. Although it is not possible to control most environmental forces, it *is* possible to convert them into opportunities or to minimize their negative impact by isolating them and attending to them in advance. In addition to identifying the force itself, an environmental scan also includes an estimate of its size, timing and duration, and, where possible, a recommendation for the organization's most productive response.

EXIT STRATEGY: A plan to divest a program, product, service or business. Exit strategies are typically prepared well in advance of implementation, which can occur for both positive and negative reasons: To convert an asset into cash; to find a home for an asset in order to increase social outcomes; or to exercise damage control, sometimes by allowing a program, product, service or business to die a natural death.

FEASIBILITY STUDIES: Used to determine whether ideas for ***earned income strategies*** or a ***social sector business*** can succeed in the marketplace. The objective is to eliminate ideas as quickly as possible to avoid wasting time on those that are not workable. A typical feasibility study makes successive passes through the surviving ideas, winnowing them each time. See ***market research*** and ***risk analysis***.

FEE-FOR-SERVICE: ***Earned income*** received in exchange for delivery of a specific unit of service. Payment may be made either by the person or organization receiving the service or by a third party such as an insurance company or, in the United States, through a public sector reimbursement program such as Medicare or Medicaid.

HYBRID BUSINESS: A ***social sector business*** that simultaneously employs the people it serves (see ***affirmative business***) and delivers a product or service that has a direct impact on a specific social need (see ***mission-driven product or service business***).

HYBRID BUSINESS CULTURE: A business culture that combines the best of both the traditional nonprofit mentality and the traditional for-profit mentality. See "Crossing the Cultural Divide"® on pages 32–33.

INDIRECT COSTS: The costs associated with a program, product, service or business that are typically "hidden" (for example, a percentage of a senior manager's time devoted to product development or marketing; or overhead costs such as rent and utilities allocated to a specific product or service). Too often, nonprofits fail to consider indirect costs when creating their business plans and therefore develop inaccurate financial projections. See also ***direct costs***.

INNOVATION: The creation of something new. Innovation is often confused with ***entrepreneurship***, but innovation does not necessarily include ***earned income***.

INNOVATORS, ENTREPRENEURS and PROFESSIONAL MANAGERS: All three are needed during the evolution of a successful ***social enterprise***, but in sequence – and few people excel in more than one of the three areas. *Innovators* develop and field-test prototypes; ***entrepreneurs*** turn those prototypes into businesses; and *professional managers* develop and install whatever infrastructure is needed to secure the future.

MARKETING: Marketing is *not* a business function – it *is* the business, and it begins with decisions about what products and services to offer (see ***strategic marketing***) and what ***target markets*** to pursue. See ***entrepreneurial strategic planning***, ***marketing plan*** and ***tactical marketing***.

MARKETING COMMUNICATIONS: One of the four parts of the ***marketing mix***. The goal of marketing communications is to convey key messages to ***target markets***, and the primary techniques are advertising, publicity, personal selling and sales promotion.

MARKETING MIX: See ***tactical marketing***.

MARKETING PLAN: Development of a marketing plan begins with the answers to five questions, and the purpose of ***marketing*** is to close the gap between the answers to questions four and five:

- What must happen for the organization to be successful?
- Who must be involved?
- What must they do?
- What must they *believe* before they will do it?
- What do they believe *now*?

The goal of marketing, therefore, is to win a share of ***client***, ***customer*** or ***stakeholder*** mind, and the people being targeted must be led through four stages:

- *Awareness* (getting their attention)
- *Understanding* (making sure they comprehend what the organization is saying – and what it is *not* saying)
- *Credibility* (do they *believe* what the organization is saying?)
- *Persuasion* (in the light of equally credible claims from others, will they do what the organization needs it to do?)

The marketing team will need to develop appropriate ***positioning strategies*** and use a variety of ***tactical marketing*** weapons to guide its clients, customers and stakeholders through the process. However, there are at least four major obstacles to creating a successful marketing plan:

- Lack of commitment by senior management
- No written plan
- Failure to involve the people charged with carrying out the plan
- A lack of quantified objectives

MARKETING RESEARCH: Unlike ***market research***, which investigates the viability of a specific product, service or market segment, marketing research evaluates the effectiveness of an organization's packaging, ***pricing strategies***, distribution and

marketing communications strategies. See ***tactical marketing***.

MARKET PULL and MARKET PUSH: If a ***social enterprise*** starts with its current products and services and then tries to find somebody willing to pay for them, it will be trying to *push* itself into the market. However, if the business starts with its potential ***customers***, discovers what they need and are willing to pay for, and then builds it, the customers will *pull* it into the market and significantly increase its chances for long-term success. The preferred approach, therefore, is to begin the process with thorough ***market research***. However, if a business is introducing a product or service to the commercial market that has never been offered there before, then the research may not be conclusive and market push might be the only alternative.

MARKET RESEARCH: Intelligent decisions about what products or services to offer and what ***target markets*** to pursue can only be made after thorough research, which typically occurs in two stages:

- *Secondary research* is designed to gather as much information as possible from existing documents (such as articles, brochures and reports)

- Once the list of possibilities has been narrowed by secondary research, *primary research* consists of face-to-face conversations with past and potential customers

The goal during both stages is to eliminate possibilities as quickly as possible in order to avoid unnecessary time and expense.

The first step in market research is ***market segmentation***. The next steps are to answer a series of questions about each segment:

- How many people in the segment actually need the product or service, regardless of their ability to pay? And how critical is their need?

- What are the ***critical success factors*** associated with designing, developing and delivering the product or service for this particular segment?

- What ***environmental forces*** will play a role? When will they occur? Will they be positive or negative? How helpful or damaging will they be? Do we have the capability to capitalize on the opportunities and mitigate the threats?

- Who are the primary competitors? How do we rank against them in terms of critical success factors and environmental forces? Can we win?

- What is the potential size of the segment in terms of dollars? And what is the opportunity within the segment? Is it growing, remaining flat or declining? How much has been exploited? How much of the competition's share is vulnerable?

- What are the fixed and variable costs? Will we make a profit or lose money? How much?

MARKET SEGMENTATION: Every business has both a "subject" and a "predicate" – a specific product or service aimed at one or more specific ***target markets*** (for example, "tutoring services *for* potential high school dropouts" or "computer training *for* men and women on welfare"). Dividing mass markets into smaller components is called "market segmentation," and the criteria for dividing a consumer market could include such things as geography (*e.g.*, nations, states, regions, counties, cities, neighborhoods, climates); demographics (*e.g.*, age, income, gender, marital status, family size, occupation, education, income, nationality); psychographics (*e.g.*, customer lifestyles, activities, interests, social class, personality characteristics, political leanings); or the way customers behave toward a specific product or service (*e.g.*, frequency of purchase, sensitivity toward price, levels of desired quality, and so on). For an industrial market, segmentation could be based on such things as the type of end user, the size of the customer, the cost of distribution, or many other factors.

MISSION-DRIVEN PRODUCT OR SERVICE BUSINESS: Unlike an ***affirmative business***, which *employs* the people served by a ***social enterprise***, a mission-driven product or service business generates revenue from the delivery of a product or service *to* the people being served, although payment may come from a third party such as a government agency or entitlement program or from a private insurance company. Examples include such things as hospice care, tutoring services for potential high school dropouts, assistive devices for people who are physically challenged, and personal care services for elderly people. See ***hybrid business***.

NICHE MENTALITY: A business approach that emphasizes specific products or services aimed at specific ***target markets*** rather than trying to be all things to all people.

NONPROFIT BUSINESS VENTURE: See ***social sector business***.

NONPROFIT ENTREPRENEUR: An individual who pays increasing attention to market forces without losing sight of the nonprofit's underlying mission. See ***social enterprise, social entrepreneur*** and ***double bottom line***.

OPERATIONAL PHILANTHROPY: Operational philanthropy occurs when a nonprofit becomes an *integral* part of a commercial company's business activity by acting as a manufacturing sub-contractor (see ***cause-related purchasing***) or by serving as one of the company's distributors. In essence, the commercial company creates a business relationship with a nonprofit instead of giving it a grant – *and therefore becomes dependent on the nonprofit's performance for its own success*. The phrase was coined by Gary Mulhair of Pioneer Human Services in 1997, and operational philanthropy is one of the four most powerful types of strategic partnerships between a commercial company and a nonprofit. See also ***cause-related marketing, distributor relationships*** and ***supplier relationships***.

ORGANIZATIONAL CULTURE: The (often unspoken) compacts that enable the members of an organization to understand why it exists, who it serves and how to serve them. The precepts of the organization's culture determine the perceptions and behaviors of its members, both positively and negatively.

ORGANIZED ABANDONMENT: A term coined by Peter Drucker to encourage nonprofits to eliminate programs, products and services that are no longer needed, are no longer competitive, or no longer fit their mission. "The Organized Abandonment Grid"®, created by Jerr Boschee (see page 19), operationalizes Drucker's insights. See ***entrepreneurial strategic planning***.

POSITIONING STRATEGIES: The tools an organization uses to differentiate itself from its competitors *in the minds* of its ***clients***, ***customers*** and other ***stakeholders***. Each organization must develop an overall positioning strategy and complementary strategies for each of its programs, products and services. At the overall level, success or failure begins and ends with the organization's image, and every organization has an image whether it wants one or not – the only question is whether it will help shape the image (see ***marketing plan***) or leave the shaping to others. The stakes are high: A positive image is hard to achieve, and even harder to regain once it is lost. It enhances employee morale, gives donors additional confidence, improves community relations, lowers the cost of sales, makes higher prices palatable, speeds market penetration, builds customer loyalty, and enhances recruitment of employees. At the program, product and service level, developing a positioning strategy is a three-step process: Discovering what people think are the most important dimensions of the program, product or service (***market research***); building them in; and then telling clients, customers and stakeholders what has been done (***marketing communications***).

PRICING STRATEGIES: One of the four parts of the ***marketing mix***. The most common pricing strategies are "penetration" (low) pricing (typically used when introducing a new product or service or to build market share); "prestige" (high) pricing (to establish a reputation for quality); "value" pricing, which rises or falls according to market demand; "cost-oriented" pricing (typically used to achieve a specific profit margin or return on investment; and "psychological" pricing (*e.g.*, discounts and flexible payment plans).

PUBLIC SECTOR SUBSIDIES: Payments to nonprofits by the public sector that are not tied to a specific *quid pro quo*. See ***earned income***.

RESEARCH AND DEVELOPMENT (R&D): An often overlooked expenditure essential for a ***social enterprise*** to remain competitive, either by improving its existing products and services, developing new ones, changing its ***target markets***, or adjusting its ***marketing plans***. See ***market research***.

RETURN ON INVESTMENT: Financial return on investment (FROI) is concerned with the cash flow, profitability, balance sheet and other financial results necessary for an ***earned income strategy*** or a ***social sector business*** to be deemed successful. Social return on investment (SROI) is concerned with the social outcomes of the strategy or business, and environmental return on investment (EROI) is concerned with the environmental impact. In all three areas, the possible returns will differ depending on the type of strategy or business – and the definition of "success" will vary from organization to organization.

RISK ANALYSIS: A thorough analysis of risks – along with an outline of planned responses – can be the most credible part of a ***business plan***.

SCREENING CRITERIA: In order to sift through the many possible ideas for a ***social sector business***, the members of a nonprofit's ***entrepreneurial planning team*** should identify five to seven criteria that capture the parameters of a *perfect* business venture for *their* organization (*e.g.*, capital constraints, required expertise, ideal market conditions, competitive strengths, favorable ***environmental forces***).

SELF-SUFFICIENCY: The ability to fund the future of a nonprofit through ***earned income*** *alone* – without having to depend in whole or in part on charitable contributions or ***public sector subsidies***.

SEPARATION STRATEGY: A ***social sector business*** started by a nonprofit will have a better chance to succeed if it is separated as much as possible from its parent. In his book *Managing for Profit in the Nonprofit World*, Paul Firstenberg writes: "The greater the separation in terms of form, staffing, oversight, and location, the greater are the chances that the profit-making component will be able to function with the necessary clarity of purpose and operating style appropriate to its objectives." Although it is reasonable to incubate the business internally for a short period of time, the sooner and more completely it can be separated, the better its chances for success. Among other things, separation might require the business to adopt a different name, seek a different location, recruit a different type of employee, and install radically different incentive packages.

SOCIAL ENTERPRISE: Any organization, in any sector, that uses ***earned income strategies*** to pursue a ***double bottom line*** or a ***triple bottom line***, either alone (as a ***social sector business***) or as part of a mixed revenue stream that includes charitable contributions and ***public sector subsidies***.

SOCIAL ENTREPRENEUR: Any person, in any sector, who runs a ***social enterprise***.

SOCIAL ENTREPRENEURSHIP: The art of simultaneously pursuing both a financial and a social ***return on investment*** (the ***double bottom line***).

SOCIAL FIRM: See ***affirmative business***.

SOCIAL INVESTING: Occurs when individuals or institutions combine their financial objectives with a commitment to social concerns such as social justice, economic development, peace or a healthy environment. See ***double bottom line*** and ***triple bottom line***.

SOCIALLY RESPONSIBLE BUSINESS: See ***corporate social responsibility.***

SOCIAL SECTOR BUSINESS: A business designed to *directly* address a social need and simultaneously make a profit through ***earned income*** alone, regardless of whether it is structured as a for-profit or nonprofit entity.

STAKEHOLDER: Any person, group or institution with an impact on an organization or affected by it.

STRATEGIC FRAMEWORK: Every organization, in any sector, must create and constantly refine a strategic framework for its activities. The framework consists of the answers to five questions:

- *What is our vision*? How do we want the world to change?
- *What is our mission?* What will we do to bring about that change?
- *What are the core values that will guide us?* What do we stand for?
- *What are our long-term goals*? What outcomes are we seeking?

- *What will be our primary strategies*? How will we reach our goals?

STRATEGIC MARKETING: There are six fundamental strategic marketing questions (see also ***tactical marketing***):

- Who are our ***customers***?
- What do they want/need/value?
- Can *we* provide it?
- *Should* we provide it?
- How can we differentiate ourselves from our competitors?
- Can we *win*?

STRATEGIC PARTNERSHIPS: Entrepreneurial alliances between nonprofits and commercial companies. See ***cause-related marketing, distributor relationships, operational philanthropy*** and ***supplier relationships***.

STRATEGIC PHILANTHROPY: See ***venture philanthropy***.

SUPPLIER RELATIONSHIPS: Supplier relationships take place when either a nonprofit or a commercial company supplies personnel, raw materials and/or finished components to the other. They are one of the four most powerful types of strategic partnerships between a commercial company and a nonprofit. See ***cause-related marketing, distributor relationships*** and ***operational philanthropy***.

SUSTAINABILITY: The ability to fund the future of a nonprofit through a *combination* of ***earned income***, charitable contributions and ***public sector subsidies***.

SUSTAINABLE DEVELOPMENT: Community and economic development that meets the needs of the present without compromising the ability of future generations to meet their own needs.

TACTICAL MARKETING: Once an organization has answered its key ***strategic marketing*** questions, it must adopt whatever tactics are necessary to sway its ***clients, customers*** and other ***stakeholders***. The four tactical marketing weapons are known collectively as the ***marketing mix***: "Packaging" (product or service design), ***pricing strategies, distribution channels*** and ***marketing communications***.

TARGET MARKETS: The segments of a mass market that have the most potential for a specific product or service. See ***market segmentation***.

TRIPLE BOTTOM LINE: The simultaneous pursuit of ***return on investment*** in three areas – financial, social and environmental. See ***double bottom line***.

UNRELATED BUSINESS INCOME: ***Earned income*** derived from products or services not *directly* related to the charitable purpose of a nonprofit, including income from the organization's under-utilized assets (such as facility downtime) or as conveniences for its clients or patrons (such as parking lots or cafeterias). In the United States, unrelated business income is subject to taxation and, at significant levels in proportion to total income, may jeopardize a nonprofit's tax-exempt status.

VALUE RUBS: When two or more of a ***social enterprise's*** economic, social and environmental bottom lines are in conflict and decisions must be made that may temporarily or permanently disrupt the existing balance.

VENTURE CAPITAL: The money and resources made available to startup firms and small businesses with exceptional growth potential. It typically comes in stages:

- *Angel money:* Used to convert an idea into a prototype, which is the most difficult and expensive money to raise because it is sought and needed before management can prove the product or service can be produced and distributed at a competitive price. Angel money frequently comes from friends, relatives, business acquaintances and others who believe in an entrepreneur's abilities or idea and are willing to invest significant sums of money long before the business is established.

- *Seed capital:* Used to test market a working or almost-working prototype to make sure it can be produced and delivered at a cost that allows the company to make a profit.

- *First-stage financing:* Used to help the company begin selling and delivering its product or service, but not to cover market expansion, risk reduction or acquisition costs.

- *Second-stage financing:* Used to expand the company's marketing efforts and provide whatever working capital is needed to fuel the company's growth.

- *Mezzanine (or third-stage) financing:* Typically the last round of financing prior to an initial public offering.

VENTURE PHILANTHROPY: The application by donors and investors of certain principles traditionally associated with venture capitalists to improve the capacity or performance of a nonprofit or to invest in a ***social sector business***. Key elements typically include a combination of cash and expertise, including long-term funding relationships (three to six years), more direct engagement and problem-solving with leadership, development of more detailed ***business plans***, performance monitoring, and an ***exit strategy***.

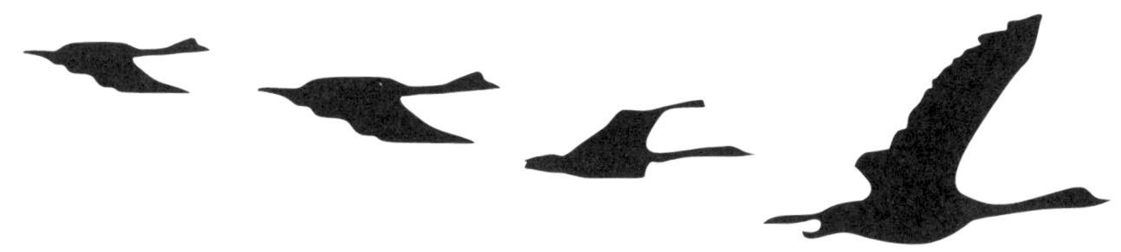

SECTION THREE

Selected bibliography (print and electronic)

Selected Bibliography: Print

Alter, Sutia Kim. *Managing the Double Bottom Line: A Business Planning Guide for Social Enterprises.* Washington, D.C.: Save The Children, 2000.

See also *www.virtueventures.com/setypology/semg.aspx* for Kim Alter's "social enterprise typology"

Austin, James E. *The Collaboration Challenge: How Nonprofits and Businesses Succeed Through Strategic Alliances.* San Francisco: Jossey-Bass Publishers, 2000

Barker, Joel Arthur. *Paradigms: The Business of Discovering the Future.* New York: HarperBusiness, A Division of HarperCollins Publishers, 1993

Boschee, Jerr. "Keep or Kill? Score Your Programs: Use This Tool to Decide Which Activities to Nurture – and Which to Abandon," Nonprofit World, September-October 2003, pp. 12-15.

Boschee, Jerr. *The Social Enterprise Sourcebook.* Minneapolis: Northland Institute, 2001

Brattina, Anita F. *Diary of a Small Business Owner: A Personal Account of How I Built a Profitable Business.* New York: American Management Association, 1996

Brinckerhoff, Peter C. *Social Entrepreneurship: The Art of Mission-Based Venture Development.* New York: John Wiley & Sons, Inc., 2000

Bygrave, William D. *The Portable MBA in Entrepreneurship, 3rd Edition.* New York: John Wiley & Sons, Inc., 2003

Collins, James C., and Jerry I. Porras. *Built to Last: Successful Habits of Visionary Companies.* New York: HarperCollins Publishers, Inc., 2004

Davis, Lee, and Nicole Etchart. *Profits for Nonprofits: An Assessment of the Challenges in NGO Self-Financing.* Providencia, Santiago, Chile: Nonprofit Enterprise and Self-sustainability Team (NESsT), 1999

Dees, J. Gregory, Jed Emerson and Peter Economy. *Enterprising Nonprofits: A Toolkit for Social Entrepreneurs.* New York: John Wiley & Sons, Inc., 2001

Dees, J. Gregory, Jed Emerson and Peter Economy. *Strategic Tools for Social Entrepreneurs: Enhancing the Performance of Your Enterprising Nonprofit.* New York: John Wiley & Sons, Inc., 2002

DuRand, John. *The Affirmative Enterprise.* St. Paul, MN: MDI Press, 1990

Emerson, Jed, and Fay Twersky. *New Social Entrepreneurs: The Success, Challenge and Lessons of Non-profit Enterprise Creation.* San Francisco: Roberts Foundation, Homeless Economic Development Fund, 1996

Firstenberg, Paul B. *Managing for Profit in the Nonprofit World.* New York: The Foundation Center, 1986

Hawken, Paul. *Growing a Business.* New York: Simon & Schuster, 1988

Kotler, Philip and Alan R. Andreasen. *Strategic Marketing for Nonprofit Organizations (Sixth Edition).* New York: Prentice-Hall, Inc., 2002

Larson, Rolfe. *Venture Forth! The Essential Guide to Starting a Moneymaking Business in Your Nonprofit Organization.* St. Paul, Minnesota: Amherst H. Wilder Foundation, 2002

McLaughlin, Thomas A. *Nonprofit Mergers and Alliances: A Strategic Planning Guide.* New York: John Wiley & Sons, Inc., 1998

Nicholls, Dr. Alex, ed. *Social Entrepreneurship: New Paradigms of Sustainable Social Change.* Oxford: Oxford University Press, 2006

Nonprofit Enterprise and Self-sustainability Team. *Get Ready, Get Set: Starting Down the Road to Self-Financing.* Providencia, Santiago, Chile: Nonprofit Enterprise and Self-sustainability Team (NESsT), 2004

Nonprofit Enterprise and Self-sustainability Team. *The NGO-Business Hybrid: Is the Private Sector the Answer?* Washington, DC: The Program on Social Change and Development, School of Advanced International Studies, Johns Hopkins University, 1997

Nonprofit Enterprise and Self-sustainability Team. *Risky Business: The Impacts of Merging Mission and Market.* Providencia, Santiago, Chile: Nonprofit Enterprise and Self-sustainability Team (NESsT), 2004

Robinson, Andy. *Selling Social Change (Without Selling Out).* San Francisco: Jossey-Bass, 2002

Shore, Bill. *Revolution of the Heart: A New Strategy for Creating Wealth and Meaningful Change.* New York: Riverhead Books, published by The Berkeley Publishing Group, 1995

Shore, Bill. *The Cathedral Within: Transforming Your Life by Giving Something Back.* New York: Random House, 1999

Skloot, Edward (editor). *The Nonprofit Entrepreneur: Creating Ventures to Earn Income.* New York: The Foundation Center, 1988

Steckel, Dr. Richard, with Robin Simons and Peter Lengsfelder. *Filthy Rich & Other Nonprofit Fantasies: Changing the Way Nonprofits Do Business in the '90s.* Berkeley, CA: Ten Speed Press, 1989

Steckel, Dr. Richard, Robin Simons, Jeffrey Simons and Norman Tanen. *Making Money While Making a Difference: How to Profit with a Nonprofit Partner.* Homewood, Illinois: High Tide Press, Inc., 1999

Trout, Jack, and Al Reis. *The 22 Immutable Laws of Marketing.* New York: HarperCollins Publishers, Inc., 1994

SELECTED BIBLIOGRAPHY: ELECTRONIC

Ashoka: Innovators for the Public: *www.ashoka.org* • More than 1,500 Ashoka Fellows in 53 countries are developing systemic-changing organizations in the areas of economic development, health, environment, education, human rights and civic participation. Ashoka currently chooses and finances about 150 new Fellows each year and also publishes *Changemakers,* an online journal that focuses on social entrepreneurship around the world.

Blended value: *www.blendedvalue.org* • A discussion of blended value in five areas: Corporate social responsibility, social enterprise, social investing, strategic philanthropy and sustainable development. Also includes a list of web resources, books, articles, and papers.

The Chronicle of Philanthropy: *www.philanthropy.com* • A bi-weekly newspaper covering the world of philanthropy, with frequent articles about social entrepreneurs.

Community Wealth Ventures, Inc.: *www.communitywealth.org* • Helps nonprofits create business ventures and corporate partnerships. Also helps corporations design and implement community investment strategies.

"Enterprising Nonprofits: Revenue Generation in the Nonprofit Sector": *www.ventures.yale.edu/factsfigures.asp* • A detailed summary by Cynthia W. Massarsky and Samantha L. Beinhacker describing a national research project that examines social enterprise activity in the United States.

The Institute for Social Entrepreneurs: *www.socialent.org* • Provides seminars, workshops and consulting services for social entrepreneurs in the United States and elsewhere. Jerr Boschee is the Founder and Executive Director.

National Center on Nonprofit Enterprise (NCNE): *www.nationalcne.org* • A consortium of colleges and universities created to help nonprofits make wise economic decisions by bringing together leading scholars, academic researchers, business leaders and economic decision-makers to focus on key issues.

Nonprofit Enterprise and Self-sustainability Team (NESsT): *www.nesst.org* • Develops social enterprises in emerging democracies worldwide through a philanthropic investment fund, consulting services, publications, workshops, and an online global shopping portal that helps social enterprises reach a wider consumer market for their products and services.

***The NonProfit Times*:** *www.nptimes.com* • A bi-weekly newspaper specializing in nonprofit management.

Nonprofit World: *www.snpo.org* • A bi-monthly magazine published by the Society for Nonprofit Organizations that focuses on nonprofit leadership, management and governance issues.

npEnterprise Forum: *www.npEnterprise.net* • The official listserv of the Social Enterprise Alliance *(see below)*, with thousands of participants worldwide.

Roberts Enterprise Development Fund (REDF): *www.redf.org* • Provides guidance, leadership, financial support and training to a portfolio of social enterprises in the San Francisco Bay area that employ people who face poverty, homelessness, mental illness and other barriers to employment. REDF also publishes numerous reports about its work and has pioneered the development of tools to measure social return on investment (SROI).

Schwab Foundation for Social Entrepreneurship (Geneva): *www.schwabfound.org* • Creates international networks of successful social entrepreneurs and mobilizes the financial and in-kind resources they need to expand.

Skoll Centre for Social Entrepreneurship, Said Business School, Oxford University: *www.sbs.ox.ac.uk/html/faculty_skoll_main.asp* • Promotes social entrepreneurship worldwide by sponsoring the annual Skoll World Forum on Social Entrepreneurship, conducting research, and providing fellowships for MBA students specializing in social entrepreneurship.

Skoll Foundation: *www.skollfoundation.org* • The Skoll Awards for Social Entrepreneurship support the work of established social entrepreneurs around the world. The Foundation also sponsors the Social Edge listserv and has created a public television documentary series hosted by Robert Redford that showcases the work of 12 social entrepreneurs in eight countries.

Social Capital Partners (Canada): *www.socialcapitalpartners.ca* • Invests in Canadian social enterprises that employ people who live outside the economic mainstream.

Social Enterprise Alliance: *www.se-alliance.org* • The leading membership organization for social entrepreneurs in the United States, and the only one devoted exclusively to building sustainable nonprofits through earned income strategies. Its conference for social entrepreneurs is the largest of its kind in the world, and it also provides a variety of other education and technical assistance. Most Alliance members are nonprofit practitioners and grant-makers, but also include management consultants, for-profit businesses and academics. Practitioner members range from early stage entrepreneurs seeking the nuts and bolts knowledge to start and run an earned income activity to well-established practitioners seeking an opportunity to exchange ideas with other leaders in the field.

***Social Enterprise Reporter*:** *www.sereporter.com* • An online monthly magazine devoted exclusively to social enterprise.

Social Venture Network (SVN): *www.svn.org* • Promotes new models and leadership for socially and environmentally sustainable business through member initiatives, information services and community forums. SVN hosts two conferences each year, one for its members and one for its members and invited guests. SVN Europe and SVN Asia are sister organizations.

The School for Social Entrepreneurs (England): *www.sse.org.uk* • A program for social entrepreneurs that includes a growing network of schools throughout the United Kingdom.

Workability International: *www.workability-international.org* • Headquartered in the U.K., its 66 members in 27 countries employ more than two million people who have disabilities. Hosts an annual conference for its members in a different country each year.

JERR BOSCHEE has been an advisor to social entrepreneurs in the United States and elsewhere for more than 25 years.

To date he has been a keynoter or conducted master classes in 41 states and 14 countries and has long been recognized as one of the founders of the social enterprise movement worldwide.

Mr. Boschee is Executive Director of The Institute for Social Entrepreneurs, based in Minnesota, which he created in 1999, and is Chairman and CEO of Peace Corps Encore!, a nonprofit he co-founded in 2003 to send former Peace Corps Volunteers and staff members back into service on short-term assignments that match their professional expertise with specific social needs.

He is the former President and CEO of The National Center for Social Entrepreneurs, is one of the six co-founders of the Social Enterprise Alliance, and was named by *The NonProfit Times* to both its 2004 and 2005 nonprofit sector "Power & Influence Top 50" lists.

Mr. Boschee served from 2001 to 2004 as an advisor to England's Department of Trade and Industry Social Enterprise Unit, is the co-editor of *A Reader in Social Enterprise* (2000), and is the author of *The Social Enterprise Sourcebook* (2001). He has served as a guest lecturer at numerous academic institutions, including the Said Business School at the University of Oxford, the Judge School of Management at the University of Cambridge, Duke University, The Kellogg School of Management at Northwestern University, Stanford University, the Carlson School of Management at the University of Minnesota, and many others.

Mr. Boschee has also been a General Manager for a Fortune 100 company, Managing Editor for a chain of 44 newspapers, and a Peace Corps Volunteer in India.